HEART, MIND, AND STRENGTH

Theory and Practice for Congregational Leadership

HEART, MIND, AND STRENGTH

Theory and Practice for Congregational Leadership

Jeffrey D. Jones

Foreword by Peter J. Gomes

THE ALBAN INSTITUTE

Herndon, Virginia
www.alban.org

The Alban Institute
2121 Cooperative Way, Suite 100
Herndon, VA 20171-5370
www.alban.org

Unless otherwise noted, all Scripture quotations are from the New Revised Standard Version of the Bible, copyright © 1989, Division of Christian Education of the National Council of the Churches of Christ in the United States of America, and are used by permission.

Scripture quotations marked RSV are from the Revised Standard Version of the Bible, copyright © 1946, 1952, and 1972 by the Division of Christian Education of the National Council of the Churches in the United States of America, and are used by permission.

Cover design by Tobias Becker, Bird Box Design.

Library of Congress Cataloging-in-Publication Data

Jones, Jeffrey D.
  Heart, mind, and strength : theory and practice for congregational leadership / Jeffrey D. Jones.
       p. cm.
  Includes bibliographical references (p. 167).
  ISBN 978-1-56699-380-7
  1. Christian leadership. I. Title.

BV652.1.J65 2008
253—dc22
                              2008040927

08   09   10   11   12   VP   5   4   3   2   1

Table of Contents

Foreword

The Reverend Dr. Jeffrey D. Jones has written an exceptional book, *Heart, Mind, and Strength: Theory and Practice for Congregational Leadership*, that is certain to appeal to those who lead, teach, and interact within the congregational setting. In it he invites the reader to see leadership in terms of two seemingly conflicting statements: "It's never about you" and "It's always about you," and to come to terms with those "seemingly conflicting realities if we are to be both effective and faithful leaders." By focusing our attention on Christ and the church, he hopes to inform our understanding of ourselves as Christ's disciples and to share theoretical and practical insights into the various facets of leadership. Of those facets, he identifies two as primary, which he calls "the 'who' and the 'what' of leadership." The 'who' of leadership includes dimensions such as our spiritual life, the depth of our relationship with Christ, and our own self-knowledge; it is a "product of our own continuing growth both as people and as leaders," and it is always paired with the 'what' of leadership.

Leadership, says Dr. Jones, is about change and about power, especially now, when the global community is continually shifting and eddying as the disposition of information becomes instantaneous and people frequently react without adequate time for reflection. Congregational leaders have a "specific responsibility to . . . enhance the quality of both the skill and the art we bring to our leadership," he notes, which must continually evolve. Leadership, he also notes, is about relationships—always.

Dr. Jones states that his purpose in this book is to bring together some of the most insightful writing about congregational leadership and apply it to the use of the congregational leader of today. He speaks of "congregational leadership," "the practices of congregational leadership," and of "leadership and power," and pinpoints three perspectives on leadership to shape the discussion: servanthood, change, and style.

In this useful work, Dr. Jones cites myriad theologians and writers highly regarded in their various vocations, and uses their talents as examples of persuasive leadership in enhancing the ability of "those who follow to participate in God's mission in the world." Jones observes that "persuasion was at the heart of Jesus's ministry," as it was in his teaching style.

When Dr. Jones addresses the topic of relationships and their centrality to leadership, he points out that "how people feel about you"—the leader—"is just as important as what they think about you, especially when it comes to their decision about whether or not to follow you." He adds, "If people do not trust you, they have no reason to follow you," emphasizing that the nature of the Trinity is relational, the community of Christ based on relationships.

Modeling faithfulness, the author continues, is modeling values and authenticity, and "giving insight for practicing a good, moral, and upright life so we can provide a picture of what we strive to achieve." When we model faithfulness we model "kingdom values" and "kingdom ways." The psalms provide a model of honest and authentic faith.

The concept of vision—the "vision thing," as is colloquially said today—threads throughout the book, in the sense of its importance for institutions both sacred and secular and the fact that there are as vast differences in the understanding of it as there are among peoples and strategic planning processes. The essential affirmation is that "for the church, the vision is always God's," and the key is how God's vision is discerned. Dr. Jones illuminates the definition of vision by saying that it "may vary from writer to writer . . . [but that] for our purposes it is enough to say that vision is a congregation's preferred picture of the future."

In the middle section of the book, Dr. Jones takes up the creation and sustenance of common ground, learning to empower others by using tools readily at hand, and he pinpoints ways in which the congregational leader actually works with groups. In sum, he describes ways in which institutional conflict and stress may be utilized, such as in the role those emotions play in organizational change. "Ministry in all its forms is a wondrous thing," he tells the reader, making great demands on both clergy and laity and "at the same time bestowing wondrous gifts."

Dr. Jones leaves us with the thought that "Our ministry in the church is no exception . . ." and an "impossible challenge:"

> . . . yet if we attend to the "who" and the "what," if we nurture both the heart and the mind, the strength we need for the challenges we face will come to us. By the grace of God, it will come.

Dr. Jeffrey Jones's previously stated purpose in the book was to bring together some of the most enlightened and insightful writing about congregational leadership and offer it for the use of congregational leaders today, and he has done so successfully, with erudition and creativity. That he is eminently qualified needs no elucidation, as he is author of more than five books and has served a number of parishes, including his present church in Plymouth, Massachusetts. In The First Baptist Church, of which Dr. Jones is pastor and I a member, I am privileged to experience and applaud the implementation of his theories, seeing our little church as a laboratory for his ideas that work. His service as director of distance learning for Andover-Newton Theological School and as instructor in ministerial leadership on that school's faculty further speaks to the broad array of his expertise.

Heart, Mind, and Strength: Theory and Practice for Congregational Leadership provides a lasting contribution to the ongoing discussion of congregational leadership, a topic to which Dr. Jones brings fresh insights, along with those of his colleagues who have examined the subject from their varying perspectives. In sharing the results of his years of leadership, as well as of his inspiration and careful thought, Dr. Jeffrey D. Jones has given much needed and important edification to the body of church literature. We—clergy and lay leaders alike—are all beneficiaries of his thoughtful guidance.

PETER J. GOMES
Harvard University

Preface

When everything else is done, an author writes the preface. It's probably the first thing you'll read, but it's the last thing I wrote. That seems a bit odd, but because the preface is in many ways a personal reflection on the writing of the book, writing it last only makes sense. Reading it first makes equal sense if you are wondering not only what the book is about but also what the person who wrote it is like. Accordingly, I'll take advantage of this preface to introduce myself to you and talk about my reason for writing, the perspective I bring to writing, the hope I have for your reading, and the thanks I have for those who have informed, supported, and encouraged me.

My Reason

I've always been fascinated by leadership. It's something I fell into, really. I learned some functional things about church administration while I was in seminary, but no one ever talked about the broader and deeper issues of leadership. As I began to see the need to be intentional about the leadership I was providing in congregations and denominational positions, I reflected a good bit on my own life experience to see where my notions about leading might have come from.

I come from a family of leaders. Both my parents held positions of leadership most of the time I was growing up. My father served as chairman of the school board in our city. My mother was active in the church—not in the traditional women's roles, but as a deacon and church moderator. Both served as president of the state-level denominational judicatory.

During high school in the 1960s, I spent three years as a page in the United States Senate and continued working there during summers while I was in college. That gave me a firsthand exposure to an array of leadership styles and personalities exhibited by a variety of political leaders—from Lyndon Johnson to Robert Kennedy to Everett Dirksen to Strom Thurmond. Just as significant, however, was that for most of my three years as a page, I held the primary leadership position among the pages. That meant that my first intense exposure to leading was one in which I had significant responsibilities for preparing the senators' desks for each session and for responding to their needs during sessions, but I was doing these tasks with friends I went to school and socialized with. I'm convinced that reality established a clear style of leadership for me.

Over the years since seminary I have held a number of leadership positions, read a lot about leadership, and talked with many people in all sorts of leadership roles, both religious and secular. I'm still fascinated by the topic. I don't totally understand what makes for a good leader—not by a long shot—but I continue to be fascinated by learning more about it.

My Perspective

Everyone has a perspective that shapes his or her understanding of the topic at hand. In this case, my experience has given me a perspective on congregational leadership. Knowing something about that perspective will, I think, help you grasp the insights I offer in this book more effectively. Here are a few of the components of my perspective:

- I have been engaged in active ministry since I graduated from seminary in 1971. Not only is that a long time, but it has also been a time of significant change, and the demands placed upon leaders today are very different from those that prevailed when I began my ministry. I have lived through those transitions—sometimes embracing them, sometimes fighting them, but always trying to come to terms with them. So while I am attuned to the newer leadership realities, I have also experienced the transitions that are needed to adjust to those realities.

- I spent fourteen years of my ministry in national denominational work. This experience enabled me to have continuing contact with a wide range of congregations in all areas of the United States and with a great variety of theological orientations. During those years I worked to develop an approach that spoke effectively to the wide spectrum of congregations with which I had contact. That continues to be the perspective that shapes my work.

- I currently teach leadership and congregational transformation courses at a seminary. The interaction with students and colleagues, the ongoing study, the regular opportunity to organize my own thinking and experiences in a way that brings understanding to others—all these have shaped my perspective on the demands placed upon leaders in today's congregations.

- Every congregation I have served has been smaller than the one before. I know this is not a typical career path, but it has been an exceptionally rich and meaningful one for me. I have served as an associate pastor, as the senior pastor in a multistaff situation, as the sole pastor, as a part-time pastor and as an interim pastor of two churches. I serve as a half-time pastor in a congregation that averages about forty-five in Sunday morning worship attendance. I'm certain that this current experience shapes my perspective on congregational leadership. I do not write as a small-church pastor for small churches, however. Even a brief survey of congregational resources reveals that, almost without exception, books by pastors of large churches are assumed to be for everyone, while books by small-church pastors are assumed to be just for small churches. I want to challenge that assumption and make the strong case that those with experience in the small church have something to say that will benefit leaders in all congregations, no matter their size.

• Because there is a decidedly practical bent to my approach to leadership, this is a book about leadership practices. I'm a practitioner. I teach some, yes, but my primary reference point is still my life as a pastor seeking to provide faithful and effective leadership in one congregation.

My Hope

My hope is that this book will stimulate your thinking about leadership and growth as a leader. I learned a lot writing the book—for example, that when it comes to leadership, books can help us only so much. They can introduce us to some important concepts; they can sometimes put into words truths that we already know but have been unable to articulate; they can help us see the way others deal with the issues of ministry; they can inspire us to become something more than we are right now. What they cannot do is make us better leaders.

My greatest hope is that this book will inspire in you some new and meaningful ways of thinking about leadership. I hope you will begin to see the various practices of a leader as a helpful way to look at your own leadership. I hope you will learn to value the insights secular writers and theorists provide but also understand how leadership in the congregation is different. Most of all, however, I hope you will see a meaningful truth in the title of this book—that leadership is about both heart and mind and it is only as both these are nurtured that the strength we need to lead in today's congregations will come to us. The title gives it all away!

My Thanks

Every book is the product of countless people. I've done the writing, but more people than I can name have provided the inspiration. A few that are particularly important:

- Robert Greenleaf, whom I quote often in this book, cared enough about the nurturing of young leaders to write to me and meet with me regularly when I was in my early thirties and just beginning to grapple with the deeper issues of leadership.

- The congregations I have served as pastor have taught me much about leadership. Along the way I've done some good things, I think, and have also made a number of mistakes. Some have graciously put up with my less-than-stellar performance as a leader. Some, to be honest, haven't. But I have learned from both situations and am thankful.

- Sarah Drummond, my colleague at Andover Newton Theological School, is the one who first urged me to think about basing this book on leadership practices. It was a great insight and just the first of countless ways she has provided insight, encouragement, and inspiration along the way.

- Those at the Alban Institute who approached me about the possibility of writing what they called "a different kind of book on leadership" started this whole process and sent me down a road I probably would not have traveled otherwise. I thank them for the opportunity to take this journey. Beth Gaede, my editor, is what some might call "aggressive" in her editing. I mean that in the best possible sense of the word! She questions, corrects, comments, and does a whole array of things that sometimes annoyed me, but always made this a better book. I thank her for that!

- For the first time in my ministry I've found in Plymouth, Massachusetts, where I have lived for the past three years, a way to connect regularly with other clergy. A group of us meets every Wednesday morning for breakfast. Often nothing of great significance happens at those meals, but these colleagues have provided for me a profound sense of belonging and collegiality in ministry. Those who gather each Wednesday have truly been an important part of the last three years of my life and continue to play an important role in sustaining me in ministry. A monthly meeting of American Baptist pastors has also contributed in important ways to my life as a pastor. They graciously read early drafts of a few chapters of this book. The discussions we had always provided important insights, not just about my writing, but also about ministry.

- The First Baptist Church of Plymouth, which I serve as pastor, is a special place. The church is a community of genuine acceptance and caring like no other congregation I've served. The members are amazingly willing to do new things. They will try just about anything—not always without doubts and fears and maybe even reluctance, but more often than not, they are willing to give it a try. At the same time, as they well know, they have provided significant challenges for me as a leader as we attempt to face what can appear to be threats to our continued vitality as a congregation. And on top of all that, they are willing to let me talk about the life and ministry we share, as will become apparent as you read this book. It's a wondrous thing really—something that has allowed all of us to grow in faith.

- It is customary to thank one's spouse in a preface. Those who write books know full well why this is so. Writing is a consuming activity. When you add it to a schedule that is already full, it has the tendency to suck every free moment out of life. Judy, my wife, understands all that. And she puts up with it with grace and love and continuing encouragement. I am certain, however, that she, probably more than anyone, is happy the writing has come to an end and she will have a husband back again.

Plymouth, Massachusetts
July 2008

CHAPTER 1

The Who and What
of Leadership

It's never about you.
It's always about you.
This is the beginning point for our exploration of leadership in the congregation. We need to come to terms with these two seemingly conflicting realties if we are to be both effective and faithful leaders.

It's never about you. It's about Christ and the church. It's about the way in which the system as a whole is functioning. It's about those you are called to serve. It's about the need of some people to focus their anxiety on someone or something. It's about the personal issues that well up and overwhelm. It's about the state of the world. What happens to us as leaders stems from an array of issues and dynamics over which we have little or no control. We get into trouble when we forget that. We begin to take things personally or think that the reason we may be encountering resistance or not growing or finding ourselves unable to accomplish what needs to be done is that we aren't skilled or knowledgeable or faithful enough. But it's never about us.

It's always about you. You are Christ's disciple. You are part of the system and have an impact on it. You have your own anxieties. You have a personal life that shapes both your selfhood and your relationships. You are touched by events in ways that influence your life and relationships. What we accomplish as leaders depends on both our willingness and our ability to deal with whatever comes our way. We get into trouble when we forget that. We begin to think that we are victims or that the problem is "them." But it's always about us.

This book is about dealing with these two realities—developing the insight and the personhood, the skills and the gifts we need to be faithful and effective leaders. This kind of leadership is a product of both what we know and who we are. That's why it is both a skill and an art, why it is about both heart and mind. The skill of leadership comes from the development and effective use of the various "tools of the trade." The art of leadership is based in the reality that not everything a leader needs can be learned from books or reduced to a step-by-step plan that can be universally applied; rather it must come from an internal sense of the situation and what the leader brings to it.[1] It is as these come together, as we grow in both heart and mind, that the strength we need to be leaders comes to us.

What we know is important. So is who we are. No book can tell you everything you need to know—the "what" of it. And certainly no book can shape your personhood—the "who" of it. What I hope to do in this book, however, is to share some theoretical and some practical insights that can inform the "what" and influence the "who" of your leadership in positive ways.

The "What" of It

The "what" of leadership is about knowledge and skill. It has to do with techniques and processes you are aware of and how you use them. Do you know what the traits of a visionary leader or a democratic leader are, when each type of leadership is needed, and how to implement it in an appropriate manner? Do you know the difference between appreciative inquiry and asset mapping and which process might be used most effectively to help a congregation make decisions about its future? Do you understand the power dynamics of groups and the stages of group life? Can you draw on skills of conflict management to help a congregation move through the tension that change always entails?

It is easy to be overwhelmed by the "what" of it. No one person can know it all. There's always another technique that might have helped if you'd only known about it. There's always a new process that those who promote it claim will transform any organization that employs it. An exclusive focus on the "what" of leadership easily leads to a sense of inadequacy and often to a sense of guilt. When a congregation is struggling, when tensions are rising, when criticism is mounting, it's easy to think that you do not know something you should know—that if you only had greater knowledge or skill, everything would be fine.

This potential for feeling inadequate when dealing with the "what" of leadership is not a reason to give up acquiring new knowledge and developing new skills, however. Neither is it an excuse to dismiss the importance of skills and knowledge in the practice of our leadership. To lead effectively in today's congregations we need to develop an understanding of a wide variety of leadership knowledge and skills and the ability to apply these to our particular setting. These include:

- various short-term and strategic-planning processes
- an understanding of human personality, potential, and problems
- the challenges and dynamics of change
- the nature and management of conflict
- the variety of effective leader roles and their appropriateness for different settings
- systems theory and its insights into organizational behavior

- cultural and societal dynamics and their impact on congregations
- group and congregational dynamics
- team and community building

When we add to this list the array of biblical, theological, and ecclesiological knowledge and skills that are essential to leadership in the congregation, we begin to get a picture of the high demands that are placed upon all who lead.

Developing effectiveness at the "what" of leadership is a challenge, but it is one that can be met; while awareness in each of these areas is important, expertise in all of them isn't essential. Leadership in a congregation is always a team effort. If the team leader knows enough to ask the right questions and to recruit the right people, the burdens of leadership can be shared. In fact, in today's world it is essential that they be shared—not just because no one can know and do enough, but also because this is the only way the meaningful involvement essential to building broad-based commitment and enthusiasm for ministry is possible.

The "Who" of It

The "what" of leadership is only half the picture. The "who" of it matters, too. The "who" is often revealed under pressure. Your "who" is revealed in what comes out of your mouth when you need to respond instantly, without the benefit even of personal reflection. It also becomes evident in the long haul, perhaps when there's nothing dramatic going on at all—how you handle the day-to-day interactions with members of the congregation, how the way you live Monday through Saturday reflects what you preach on Sunday.

The "who" of leadership has many dimensions. Our own spiritual life and the way that affects both our self-understanding and our relationships is a primary factor. The depth of our relationship with Christ, the way that relationship is nurtured through spiritual disciplines, shapes who we are and how we relate to others in profound ways. Without that, our "who" is something less than it can be.

Another dimension of the "who" of leadership is our own self-knowledge. Years of therapy aren't essential, but a good understanding of what makes us tick is. What issues tend to threaten us? What strengths can we rely on, what blind spots can get us into trouble? How has our past experience shaped the way we relate to people? What are the needs, the hopes, the fears that drive us? All of this (and much more) influences our ability to lead. To lead effectively we need to be aware of these personal traits and the way they shape our leading. The fact is that, given a decent amount of time, almost all of them will become apparent to those we lead, so we had best be honest with ourselves right from the beginning.

The "who" of leadership also results from the way we have internalized much of the content that makes up the "what" of leadership. When that information becomes part of us, when it shapes who we are and how we relate, it becomes more than book learning. This same process is at work when a sculptor takes the knowledge of stone and the skill of stonecutting and turns a block of marble into a work of art. That knowledge and skill have been internalized in a way that allows the artist to emerge and to produce a work of art.

Craig Dykstra, vice president for religion at the Lilly Endowment, talks about the importance of the pastoral imagination in ministry. It is, he says, the "internal gyroscope" of the minister, "a way of seeing into and interpreting the world which shapes everything a pastor thinks and does." Such an imagination "requires a peculiar intelligence that involves specific capacities of mind, spirit, and action that are specific to pastoral ministry itself."[2] This is another way of describing the "who" of leadership. Yes, the pastoral imagination involves skills and knowledge, but it's something different from the knowledge that makes up the "what" of it. It is internalized knowledge—knowledge that has become part of who you are.

The "who" of leadership is a product of our own continuing growth, both as people and as leaders. It is essential, but it always needs to be paired with the "what" of leadership. The transformation in self-understanding from shepherd to liberator that Moses underwent at the burning bush formed his "who" in profound and dramatic ways. It wasn't all he needed to be an effective leader, however. He also needed the "what." For Moses, that came in the form of continuing advice from Yahweh—who initiated plagues, opened up the Red Sea, created commandments to live by. Most of us aren't fortunate enough to have God readily available to assist us directly in every leadership crisis we face. We do, however, have other sources of the knowledge we need. The books and workshops available to us are a continuing source of new knowledge and skills that can strengthen our leadership.

Faithful and effective leadership has always been about both the "what" and "who" of it. The demands of leadership in today's world, however, make awareness and nurturing of both dimensions particularly important. The massive changes that are taking place in the world—from globalization to the breakdown of Christendom to the emergence of postmodernity—shape local congregations in profound ways. We can no longer simply implement familiar plans, follow tried-and-true processes, or rely on old answers. We can no longer fall back on what we've done before and expect anything more than the continuing slow death of our congregations. All leadership today is about change. In such a time, we as congregational leaders have a specific responsibility to enhance the quality of both the skill and the art we bring to our leadership. And both need to be continually deepening, emerging, evolving, growing.

Some Additional Thoughts

My purpose in writing this book is to pull together some of the most insightful writing about leadership available today and to apply it in specific ways to the things congregational leaders do on a regular basis—the practices of their leading. Before we go further, it would be good for us to clarify a few terms I'll be using throughout the book.

Congregational Leadership

This is a book about leadership in congregations. In most cases that means the leadership of the pastor. That will be our primary concern, but not our only one. Other members of the staff, both clergy and laity, are also congregational leaders. So also are the laity who serve in the various leadership positions in the church. Additionally, in some cases laity who have no official position in the institutional structure also provide significant leadership within the congregation. This book is for all those who, because of the formal or informal authority they have been given, exert an influence on the future direction of the congregation.

Not everything I say in this book will apply to everyone. I will, for example, talk at times about the role of preaching in leadership. That, obviously, would apply to the preachers among us. Most of the content of the book, however, speaks much more broadly and can be applied to all the leadership roles I have mentioned.

Another conviction about congregational leadership that underlies this book is that leadership is always shared. No one person does it all. Sometimes the shared nature of that leadership is formalized in teams, either among the staff or including both staff and nonstaff. At other times there is no formal structure of shared leadership, but rather different people exercise leadership in different ways. Without a formal structure, for example, the pastor, the choir director, the moderator, or the board chair all exercise leadership. Whether formal or not, however, leadership in the congregation is always shared. Whether their authority is formal or not, all congregational leaders will find insights for their leading in this book.

The Practices of Congregational Leadership

This is a book about both the theory and the practice of congregational leadership. I'll be using the theories of a number of authors to provide insight for the practices in which we as leaders engage. Since our emphasis is on the practical, rather than the theoretical, I'll begin with the practices and use the theory to develop ways of being more effective in them.

What is a leadership practice? A good beginning point is the definition presented by Craig Dykstra and Dorothy Bass in *Practicing Our Faith*: "Christian practices are things Christian people do together over time in response to and in light of God's active presence for the life of the world."[3] Another way to say that might be: A Christian practice is something Christians regularly do that furthers God's mission in the world. A Christian *leadership* practice then is something Christian leaders regularly do that leads others to participate in God's mission in the world. The mission of God is about the redemption of all creation. This means, of course, that it is about salvation, healing, and wholeness (all appropriate translations of the same word in Greek), as well as the love and peace and justice that are qualities of the kingdom of God. When we participate in God's mission, we both experience those qualities ourselves and share them with others.

But is it legitimate to call the practices that are discussed in this book, which are also used in business and other secular arenas, *Christian* practices? Mark Yaconelli, who has studied and written extensively in the area of Christian practices in ministry with youth, provides an important insight here. He describes a Christian practice as "the *means* through which Christians seek to respond to God's invitations of love. They are the habits, disciplines, and patterns of life through which Christians seek communion with Christ and solidarity with others."[4] All Christian practices have the following elements: prayer, confession, the presence of the worshiping community, and solidarity with the poor.[5] The seemingly secular practices of this book, then, become Christian spiritual practices when they are imbued with these elements:

- when prayer is a vital dimension of all that we do
- when the practice causes us to look deeply at ourselves to affirm that which has been good and to admit where we have failed
- when we and the practices are intimately related to the ongoing worship life of the congregation of which we are a part
- when the practices lead others into effective and faithful participation in God's mission of the redemption of all creation

"Almost any activity," Yaconelli reminds us, "can become a spiritual practice."[6] It simply needs to embody these elements.

When our practices take on these dimensions, they become Christian spiritual practices. And when that happens, they are not only things we do in response to God's love and call. They also become ways in which we are shaped to live more faithfully as Christ's disciples. They are not only the way we respond, but also the way we are formed.

Although for purposes of this book we'll be looking at individual practices, it is important to remember that life itself is not so easily dissected and analyzed. As Dykstra and Bass point out: "In real life, however, it is very difficult to separate the practices. They flow into one another, each one making a space for God's active presence that then ripples out into other parts of life."[7] When we go deeply into any practice, it always leads us to another. We'll see that time and time again as we explore the practices in this book.

Leadership and Power

We cannot lead others to participate in God's mission in the world without exercising power. All leadership is about the use of power. If we do not understand this, we will at best fail to lead as effectively as we might. At worst, we will exercise power in perverse and abusive ways. Power can take any number of forms. It can be coercive or manipulative. It can be encouraging and persuading. But all those who have been given authority exercise power. Authority is what is granted to us by God or others. Power has to do with the way in which we use that authority to influence the actions of others.

The misuse of power is a constant temptation for leaders. This is the issue that Jesus himself had to grapple with in his second temptation (Luke 4:1–15), and it continues to confront all leaders. It is easy to think about the good we will accomplish or to trust in our own virtue to exercise power appropriately. It is easy to forget that legitimate power is never power over others, but power with and for others. We will continue to explore this issue throughout the book. At this point, however, let's note that Jesus's insight as he confronted the devil is an important one for us as well. Author and educator Parker Palmer, in his book *The Active Life*, states this clearly:

> When Jesus rejects the devil's offer of power and glory by quoting the scriptural injunction to worship and serve God alone, he is not being merely pious. . . . He is stating a simple fact: Power and glory are not the devil's to give. They belong to God alone, and only through God can we share in them.[8]

From the Christian perspective all legitimate power comes from God. It is not ours; it is God's. We can share in that power only as we participate in God's mission in the world.

In the next chapter we turn to three perspectives on leadership that will shape our discussion of the practices of congregational leadership.

CHAPTER 2

Three Perspectives on Leadership

Like the elephant in the story of the elephant and the blind men, leadership is a big animal that can be viewed from any number of perspectives. Each perspective gives us an important insight, but none presents the complete truth. Three perspectives will be particularly important for us in our exploration of leadership, so let's take some time now to become familiar with them. They are revealed in three statements about leadership.

It's about servanthood.
It's about change.
It's about style.

Perspective One: Servanthood

"The great leader is seen as servant first."[1] With those words Robert Greenleaf began what might be termed a revolution in leadership studies. The former director of management research at AT&T published his essay "The Leader as Servant" in 1970. Although it was written more than thirty-five years

ago, its insights continue to shape the discussion of leadership in the corporate, educational, nonprofit, and religious
worlds. In advocating the importance of those in positions of
authority and power serving others, Greenleaf helped shift
the discussion from the management of institutions to leadership within institutions. The previous models, which focused
on efficiency and effectiveness, began to give way to models that focused on purpose, meaning, and relationship. For
Greenleaf the true test of leadership is the impact it has on
those who are led. He wrote:

> The best test [of a leader], and difficult to administer,
> is: Do those served grow as persons? Do they, *while
> being served*, become healthier, wiser, freer, more au-
> tonomous, more likely themselves to become servants?
> *And*, what is the effect on the least privileged in society:
> will they benefit, or, at least, not be further deprived?[2]

In the business world the spirit of his writing led to the
publication of a continuing stream of books that encouraged
leaders to think about something more than the bottom line,
while also recognizing that in many situations this mindfulness would in fact improve the bottom line.[3] The insights
of servant leadership also had a significant influence in nonprofit governance and education.[4]

Despite its secular origin and focus, Greenleaf's concept of
the servant leader resonates well with biblical teaching. Jesus's
admonition to his disciples that true greatness is evidenced in
serving others (Mark 9:35) and his call to servanthood at
the Last Supper (John 13:12–16) provide clear support for
the view that any legitimate claim to leadership is based in
the ability and willingness to serve others. Greenleaf himself
attended to the religious implications of servant leadership,
most notably in the publication of "Seminary as Servant" in
1980 and "The Servant as Religious Leader" in 1982.[5]

A number of authors who have written about leadership
in the congregation acknowledge their debt to Greenleaf.

Jane Fryer, in her work on the national staff of the Lutheran Church–Missouri Synod, has written two brief books on leadership and teams and acknowledges her debt to Greenleaf.[6] David Young, who has written about and led seminars on congregational renewal, presented the concept of servant leadership as the key to renewal of the congregation.[7] Elizabeth O'Connor, from her experience with the Church of the Savior in Washington, D.C., has also written extensively about servanthood as the basis for leadership within the church and ministry within the community.[8]

Other writers, both within and outside the church, have raised serious questions about the implications of a leadership stance that focuses on servanthood.[9] They have called attention to the way in which it can be used to encourage a servant role that denies one's own personhood. They have quite rightly recognized that the concept of servanthood carries significant negative connotations, especially for those who have had a servile role forced upon them in the past. It is one thing, for example, to encourage white males, the traditional holders of power in our society, to develop a servant stance to leadership, but quite another to do so for women and members of racial/ethnic groups that have been marginalized in the past. The very word "servant" carries a powerfully different meaning for them.

As we explore the servant role of congregational leaders, it is important to recognize this reality. We will, however, continue to explore the helpful insights that Greenleaf's writing and the work of those who followed him bring to our own understanding of leadership. The following servant leadership concepts are central to the understanding of congregational leadership that we will be developing.

The Needs of Others

Leadership is always about serving the highest priority needs of those who are being led. Remember, leadership is never about you. It is always about others and their needs.

If our motivation in leading is to exercise power, if we lead so that we can feel good about what we have done for others, our claim to leadership lacks legitimacy, because we lead for what we get out of it. It's never about us. It's always about those being led. Let's be clear, however, that there is a vast difference between serving others and catering to them. The leader who is servant first is not a doormat responding to every whim and desire of those who follow. In leading, we are serving the "highest priority needs" of people and the result of this serving is that those whom we serve become "healthier, wiser, freer, more autonomous, more likely themselves to become servants." We cannot achieve these purposes simply by doing whatever people tell us to do or giving them whatever they want. It can happen only if as leaders we move beyond surface needs and demands, if we refuse to get caught in the game-playing that is so often present in organizations (including congregations), if we are willing to break the dysfunctional patterns of relationship that prevent the deepest needs from being met and significant growth from taking place. Leadership is always a risky business. When our basic orientation to leadership is serving others, we take on the responsibility of assessing the highest-priority needs of the situation and how best to serve them. We must take responsibility for acting in a way that will result in others being healthier, wiser, freer, more autonomous, more likely to become servants. Of course, we do that carefully and sensitively. We do it in conversation with others, listening deeply to them and to the various ways in which they express their needs, so that we are not simply imposing our own biases. We do it with empathy and humility. But we cannot avoid making those decisions if we are to lead effectively and faithfully. Leading this way is always risky, for we can be wrong. It can also be a very difficult thing to do when those we seek to serve are saying (either verbally or nonverbally) that they want and need something else. But it is essential.

Here's one example of how listening to deeper needs and responding to them might work. It is not unusual for members of a congregation unconsciously to send messages to visitors that they are not welcome unless they look and act like the members. This lack of welcome is often expressed in subtle ways, such as the lack of warmth with which visitors are greeted and members' neglecting to converse with them during the coffee hour. Those who engage in these behaviors can be served only by a leader who will help them face this difficult truth and grow beyond it. They may resist. They may insist that they are open and friendly to all visitors. They may insist that they do not need to change. The leader who truly serves, however, will continue to address this concern in ways that lead the members of the congregation to take responsibility for the situation, so that they can develop a fuller and more genuine practice of hospitality. In this setting, the leader uses the authority given to him or her by God and/or others to enhance the ability of those who follow to participate in God's mission in the world.

The Art of Persuasion

The servant leader leads through persuasion, using other forms of power in only the most extreme and unusual circumstances. The congregational leader is always encouraging others to take a leap of faith into more faithful living. That's a leap people must take on their own. No pushing allowed! There can be no allowance for false promises of great benefits or overstated descriptions of dire consequences, whether it be an eternity in hell or a life of unhappiness and unnecessary poverty.

A leader leads through "gentle, but clear and persistent persuasion."[10] This is the way Greenleaf describes the process of persuasion:

> One is persuaded, I believe, upon arrival at a feeling of rightness about a belief or action *through one's own intuitive sense.* One takes an intuitive step, from the closest approximation to the certainty to be reached by conscious logic (sometimes not very close), to that state in which one may say with conviction, "This is where I stand." The act of persuasion, as I limit the

definition, would help order the logic and favor the intuitive step.[11]

When we lead through persuasion then, we act as guides to those who follow. We provide the information and the modeling that allows them on their own to take the intuitive step of following.

To lead through persuasion we must have trust and patience. We need to trust that God is at work in the life of the congregation and its members, that as leaders we have attuned ourselves to that work, and that God's purposes will be achieved in God's time. When trust is present, then patience is possible. We need, of course, to be aware that sometimes what we might want to call patience is really a lack of courage or a fear of risk or just plain laziness. We'll attend to that issue a bit later. For now, let us simply affirm that coercive and manipulative power has no place in the life of a congregation. It's not that it doesn't at times produce results and the appearance of change, but rather that it does not honor the integrity of people and respect others as people created and loved by God. And from a more utilitarian perspective, without the genuine and honest commitment of the congregation to the direction in which the leader is leading, no results can last.

Persuasion was at the heart of Jesus's ministry. He was willing, for example, to let the rich young man walk away without berating him, without threatening him, without even trying again to convince him (Matt. 19:16–22). Jesus's commitment to persuasion is also clear in the teaching style he most often used. Although I have been attracted to parables as a form of teaching ever since I took a course on parables in seminary, I've only recently come to understand that one reason Jesus relied on them to teach about the kingdom of God was that in their openness and seeming absence of clear direction they provided a noncoercive means of inviting people to participate in the kingdom. Jesus didn't tell them what they needed to do or believe. Instead he told them a story and said, "Whoever has ears to hear, let them hear" (Mark 11:15, rsv), knowing full well that real listening takes more than just ears. It takes a mind and a heart as well. Parables, by their very nature, demonstrate servant leadership, because they require the listener to decide for himself or herself what their meaning is and how he or she will respond to that insight.[12]

Self-Care

The leader's ability to serve others depends upon consistent care for self. Remember, leadership is always about you.

Care for self happens in several ways. Care for our own continuing growth—becoming healthier, wiser, freer, more autonomous, more able to serve—is essential to effective and faithful leadership. It means developing new and needed skills, enhancing gifts, developing new insights into ministry and leadership

Care for self also means taking time to stop all the business and busyness of leadership—to be with family and friends, to be alone, to be with God, to care for our bodies. We all know how easy it is to keep ourselves constantly busy. We know the rationalizations we can come up with for not taking days off and for having a meeting every evening. We know that in all honesty we often take pleasure in telling others how busy we are. We will return to this topic in the next chapter, so little more needs to be said here, except this: The struggle we have in taking time for ourselves and our relationships with our families and with God is an indication that we are serving our own need to be needed, our own sense of indispensability, our own desire to be significant. It reveals that we are far from being the servant leaders God calls us to be.

When we see ourselves as servants first, our leading in the congregation takes on a whole new dimension. Our purpose in leading becomes the growth of people so that they can both experience and participate in God's mission in the world. Our use of power is shaped by a recognition of the importance of others' deciding to follow without coercion and manipulation, as well as the patience that results from trust in God's purposes. Our concern for self and our relationships with others and with God become the foundation for our ability to serve as we are called to do.

Perspective Two: Change

Leadership is always about change, especially now with the rapid and radical change that is taking place in the world. Postmodernity, the demise of Christendom, globalization, cyberspace reality, biotechnology, increased awareness of diversity, economic dislocation, emerging markets, declining industries—all these speak to the reality of the change that touches the lives of all of us and the institutions of which we are a part. To lead in today's world is to help both individuals and institutions deal with change, which inevitably means to help them change themselves. Maintaining the status quo is not an option. It is an impossibility.

In a sense this entire book is about change. The assumption that leadership is about change underlies everything we will talk about. To get us started, let's look at the work of three people who have written on the subject to gather some insights that will be particularly helpful.

Deep Change

Robert Quinn, a professor of organizational behavior at the University of Michigan, presents two clear options for institutions in today's world. Because of the degree and rate of change taking place, all organizations have a fundamental choice about their future. They can choose either deep change or slow death. There are no other options.

Deep change is "major in scope, discontinuous with the past and generally irreversible."[13] It doesn't come from rational analysis and a linear planning process. It comes only when an organization has been captured by a transforming spirit that shapes everything the organization is and does.

On the one hand, deep change seems impossible to bring about in a congregation, which because of its very nature must be the guardian of a sacred tradition. On the other hand, it is the kind of change one might naturally expect from an organization in which the Holy Spirit and its transforming power have been unleashed. Most congregations face these two conflicting realities. We are cautious about change, as well we should be, but the essence of our faith is about a radical, transforming power at work in the world to bring hope out of despair and life from death. Deep change should come naturally and eagerly for congregations, but it does not.

This kind of change is hard work. Members of the congregation must move beyond surface conversations about their reason for being to the motivations and goals that shape the life and ministry of the congregation. This difference between expressed purpose and actual purpose is one of the reasons that step-by-step vision and goal-setting processes often produce results that have little impact. In that type of planning process everything can be kept at a surface level. When you dig deeper, however, you usually discover "operative goals that often override the espoused public goals"[14] of the congregation. These operative goals determine what actually happens in an organization. These goals must change if deep change is to happen. If they are not acknowledged and dealt with, deep change is impossible. In Quinn's view, they are most often shaped by the dominant coalition in the organization/congregation—those people who through their longevity, influence, and relationships have the power and authority to set the tone of congregational life and shape the decisions the congregation makes. One of the greatest hurdles to bringing about change is that those within the dominant coalition usually believe that these operative goals are a wise and a faithful expression of the gospel. Therefore, members of this coalition do not see the necessity for deep change. In fact, they usually see deep change as a threat to everything that is sacred to them. In such circumstances, unless another group in the organization presents a different view of reality, slow death is the only alternative.

This power of the dominant coalition also determines that the motivation for change will most often come from the edges of the organization, perhaps even from outsiders. Remember, it was those from outside Jerusalem who first invited Gentiles into the community of the early church and began to question the need to maintain the Jewish law (Acts 15). The dominant coalition in Jerusalem simply didn't see the need for change. Transforming change became possible, however, when the leaders of the dominant coalition (the apostles) became aware of the need for a new understanding of what it meant to be a follower of the Way. Because of the challenge from the fringes of their group, they began to see new possibilities that would come from aligning their internal practices (requirements for membership) with the new external realities (the spread of the gospel to Gentiles). This same dynamic is at work in the congregation. Change creates conditions in which it becomes possible for those on the fringe and those on the inside to focus on the new realities they face and work together to develop a new way to respond to those realities.

There's one more thing: We cannot lead change in the congregation unless we ourselves are willing to change. New approaches to worship aren't possible unless we as worship leaders move out of our own comfort zone in leading worship. New ways of sharing ministry among clergy and laity aren't possible unless we (whether clergy or laity) are willing to give up our accustomed roles and the status and satisfaction that come with them. We cannot guide others into deeper, more faithful discipleship unless our own lives as disciples are continuing to be formed.

It truly is always about us!

Leading in a Culture of Change

Michael Fullan, who writes primarily about public education and business, brings another important dimension to our discussion of change. Rather than focusing on the process of change, he emphasizes the components essential for change. This difference may, in fact, be fairly subtle. The insight he offers, however, is vital for change in congregations.

Change, according to Fullan, is a nonlinear, usually chaotic process. "Change cannot be managed. It can be understood and perhaps led, but it cannot be controlled."[15] Given the chaotic nature of change, linear, step-by-step processes, which attempt to manage it, are problematic. They do not allow the process of change to unfold in its natural way, and they present an illusion of control that is unrealistic. Even though the proponents of those processes most often discuss their circular nature and warn against trying to follow them too rigidly, the very fact that the process is discussed in steps leads to an overly mechanistic view of organizational change.

An additional difficulty with these linear processes is that they run counter to the culture of most congregations—usually all but the largest ones, which because of their size and more hierarchical, controlling structures have developed a corporate mentality that makes the illusion of control easier to fall into. The organic nature of organizations is more apparent in most congregations, however. They really are bodies, if not always the body of Christ! There is great informality in the way decisions actually get made; there is a reliance on more casual conversation and the building of consensus. Therefore, linear planning processes placed in the hands of a few most often seem alien to congregations, if not an out-and-out imposition. People may go along, because they want to be cooperative or because they do not know what else to do. Most often, however, these step-by-step processes do not produce the desired results. We've all heard the stories about the months spent crafting a purpose statement that gets hung on the wall or printed in the Sunday worship bulletin but has no discernable impact on the ministry of the congregation—it's the kind of thing that happens when congregations rely on a linear process to enable organic change.

The difficulty a congregation has in resisting the use of a linear process is often compounded when it seeks assistance from judicatory leadership or outside consultants. Many of these people work in a corporate culture in which more disciplined planning is essential. They often rely also on being able to share usable "tools" with congregations. What they fail to recognize, however, is that what is essential for their purposes is often detrimental to congregations.

Fullan, in contrast, talks about the components of change. The challenge of leadership is to develop the various components so that they are apparent within the organization. Once that is accomplished, meaningful change can take place in its own nonlinear, often chaotic way. The components Fullan lists as essential to meaningful change are:

- moral purpose—sharing the guiding purpose for an organization's existence
- an understanding of change—developing a working knowledge of the key dimensions and dynamics of change
- relationship building—seeking relationships with diverse people and groups, especially those on the fringe and those who resist change
- creation and sharing of knowledge—sharing information in a way that it becomes usable both to initiate and to sustain change
- achievement of coherence—bringing sense and common purpose to the ambiguity that is change[16]

The presence of these components in the life of a congregation will encourage positive change. At times the change will be chaotic. At times there will be conflict. But these components set a tone that makes positive change possible.

If this approach to change were taken in a congregation, there would be no formal engagement in a step-by-step change process. Instead, these various elements would be introduced over time:

- The church board would take time on a regular basis to consider the dynamics of change in a congregation and the forces at work in the world and community that make traditional congregational approaches to ministry less effective than they once were. (For example, the board in the congregation I serve has taken a half-hour at the beginning of each of its meetings to explore issues related to change.)

- The pastor would begin to introduce concepts that underlie a vision for the congregation. (I began talking about being a disciple-forming community in my discussions with the search committee members, and when I discovered that this concept resonated well with them, began to talk about it more frequently and more broadly once I began as pastor.)

- The congregation would begin to engage in specific actions that affirmed the vision and began to actualize it. (As part of our worship, we have begun regular commissioning services, which acknowledge the ways church members are living out their lives as disciples, and pledge the church's support to them in that effort.)

- Conversations among church leaders would formalize a new understanding of the congregation's purpose and vision. (We used the development of a new church brochure that explains how we seek to be a disciple-forming community.)

- The congregation would begin to address issues of its life and ministry from the perspective of its developing understanding of the vision for the future to which God is calling it. (This concern enters the discussion as we talk about which Sunday school curriculum would work best for us, how to make visitors feel more welcome, and how we develop the annual budget. Virtually every decision we need to make can be viewed from the perspective of being a disciple-forming congregation.)

- Leaders would take every available opportunity to discuss issues related to change and vision. (I make reference to this emerging vision in sermons regularly and have developed a number of brief phrases that others in the congregation use to reinforce their own understanding of the new direction in which we are moving.)

Approaching change in this way takes time. It also takes constant attention to the ways everything in the life of a congregation can be used to further the change needed to lead the congregation more faithfully into the future.

Another insight for congregations from Fullan's work is that change involves "slow learning in context over time."[17] Meaningful and lasting change happens slowly because new answers must be discovered; it always takes time because it is related to a specific context with its unique needs, dynamics, and relationships. There are good reasons to be suspicious of quick fixes, stories of rapid growth, and programs that have worked elsewhere and come with guarantees of success. It's not that they cannot produce some change, but superficial change can often be deceiving. It may not stand the test of time. It may not be change that helps the congregation adapt to the new realities of our world, which is the focus of our next author.

Leadership without Easy Answers and Leadership on the Line

Ronald Heifetz's distinction between technical and adaptive work is profoundly important for congregations.[18] Many of us grew up in congregations in which technical work ensured effective ministry. The problems we faced were ones we understood. Either we or an outside expert could provide the answers we needed. If the Sunday school was getting smaller or it was becoming more difficult to recruit teachers, a new curriculum or enhanced teacher training was the answer. If giving declined, new stewardship campaign materials would do the trick. This is technical work. The problem is known;

the way to fix it is known—if not by us, then by an expert. The solution is just a matter of determining and applying the right solution to the problem. We can rely on "experts" to tell us what to do.

The realities most congregations face today, however, don't lend themselves to technical fixes. Often the problem with Sunday schools can no longer be solved by a new curriculum. Issues of children's learning styles, family priorities, and other factors need to be considered. Achieving an increase in giving requires more than new stewardship materials. The desire to give to specific causes, the nature of tithing as a spiritual discipline, and even the availability of online giving options need to be considered. Something other than a technical solution is needed. Most of us sense this reality, even if we haven't yet articulated it. We know we're working hard and not getting very good results. We know that the approaches that always worked don't seem to have the same impact they once did. We know we're getting tired, if not burned out, trying to make it all work. Often in such situations we look for someone to blame. We may take responsibility upon ourselves and feel guilty that we aren't able to do what we were once able to do, or that we aren't as dedicated or capable as our parents were. Or we begin to blame others—the young people who aren't as committed, the old people who are too stuck in their ways, the town soccer league that schedules games on Sunday mornings, the pastor who doesn't visit or preach or relate to people the way he or she should.

Heifetz's insights help us break out of these debilitating patterns. Because of the dramatic change taking place today, he says, many of the old answers don't work anymore. In many cases, we don't know what the new answers are. We might not even know the questions! We just know that something is not right, and we don't really know what to do about it. In this situation, Heifetz says, adaptive work is needed. We can't just apply technical fixes. Instead we need to adapt ourselves and our congregations to the new realities pressing in upon us. We can't look to experts to give us the answers. We must discover (or discern) the answers for ourselves. The "experts" we need are not those who give us the answers, but those who guide us in discovering our own answers.

Once we understand this new reality, a whole new world opens up to us. This world is one of uncertainty, a world in which significant change is essential, but also one in which new possibilities are abundant. We just need to discover them. There is no longer reason to blame ourselves or others for what seems like failure. Our difficult situation is not the result of something we or they have or haven't done. Rather, the world has changed. We have been playing the same old game by the same old rules with the same old equipment. The game may be the same, but we need to begin using the new rules and equipment. Of course, this prospect may not appeal to some who like the old way the game was played and are unsettled about having to learn new rules. However, it can also come as a great relief to many others who now at last understand what is going on and how to get back into the game.

The need to change from primarily technical to primarily adaptive work has a significant impact on the role of the leaders. One of those changes is particularly important for our purposes. Because no "expert" is available who knows the right answers, discovering (or discerning) what needs to be done becomes the work of the people (the congregation) as a whole. This means that one of the primary leadership roles in leading adaptive change is giving the work back to the people so they can accomplish it.[19] We need great confidence and fortitude for this kind of leadership! A natural and perhaps even automatic expectation of both leaders and followers is that leaders will provide the answers. If leaders don't have the answers, we might think, why should anyone follow them? If, however, no one has the answer on their own and the best answer is an adaptive one that can come only from the people themselves, a different understanding of leadership and the role leaders play in the congregation is called for. To give the work back to the people, we as leaders need to refuse to be the "answer people," even when we think we know what the answer is. We can no longer be the experts. This new approach to leading can be a great blow to one's ego. If we refuse to give answers, we may create situations in which some people think we are not doing our job. If we lead because we like having people depend upon us and the answers we give, the challenge may be even greater for us.

In truth, this is one of the most difficult lessons I've had to learn in ministry—to sit in silence when a perfectly reasonable answer is staring me in the face because it is more important that the people discover the answer themselves than that they get it quickly. And if it is truly an adaptive challenge we are facing, it's quite likely that the "perfectly reasonable answer" I see isn't the right one at all! It's not easy to make myself appear less learned, less insightful, less creative than I really am (see me winking here). But sometimes a leader needs to do precisely that to create the space in which the congregation can discover the answers that only they can discern.

At one point in my ministry, I served as interim pastor in a congregation that traditionally showed great deference to its clergy. The members had a high view of pastoral authority and deferred to the pastor on most issues related to the life and ministry of the church. I was never taken as seriously in any other church as I was here. It was great! I had never been treated so well, with so many people depending on me to tell them what to do and listening so carefully to everything I said. It's nice to be listened to. It's nice to have people follow your advice. It does wonders for the ego! What I came to realize, however, was that the recent history of this congregation included a difficult period in which members' deference to the pastor had enabled destructive behavior on his part. By constantly deferring to the pastor, the members were undercutting the great potential of their own gifts, skills, and insights. Because they constantly deferred to the pastor, they were less than the church they could be. I began responding to every question they asked me with, "What do you think?" It took about a month before their frustration had reached a level high enough that we could begin to deal with it. So at the next deacons' meeting I called attention to what I had been doing and their evident frustration. That was the beginning of a great discussion about their role and responsibility in the church. Over time, members began to claim more responsibility for their own life as a congregation. And before I left, they even acknowledged that their previous deference to the pastor had contributed to the problem that had developed. My refusal to give answers caused great frustration among the congregation's leaders. Some of the congregation probably thought I wasn't very capable and not a very good leader. But, in refusing to provide the answers, in giving the problem back to the people, I helped create a setting in which adaptive change was possible.

It's important to acknowledge at this point that not every issue should be treated from the perspective of adaptive change. Some answers are known. The basic management of the church office, building maintenance, choir rehearsals, board and committee meetings—these dimensions of congregational life continue to be fairly straightforward. The type of music the choir will sing may be an issue of adaptive change related to the desire of the congregation to reach new people, but rehearsal itself is still a technical issue. Many problems congregations encounter today can be resolved with technical responses. What we can no longer do, however, is to assume that all problems can be resolved in this way. One of the important new challenges for congregational leaders today is discerning which type of response is needed.

Technical responses are still appropriate for congregations also because discovering adaptive responses is hard work. It takes time. It always involves stress and often results in conflict. There are limits to the amount of adaptive work any organization can undertake at one time. How much is appropriate for a congregation depends on its ability to handle stress, the quality of relationships, and the level of trust between leaders and members. But there are limits for every congregation. It will always be necessary to seek technical responses to some issues that could call for adaptive change. The leadership challenge amid this reality is to focus on those issues in which adaptive change is most possible and will have the most significant impact.

All leadership is about change. Even trying to maintain the status quo in a rapidly changing world requires constant adaptation! More than that, however, if congregations are to remain attentive to the "new thing" God is doing in their midst, if they are seeking to grow in their faithfulness, change is essential. The authors we have looked at in this perspective on leadership have helped us understand that "deep" change is essential, that it is often chaotic and cannot be controlled by a linear and logical process, and that adapting to new realities requires broad involvement of a wide range of people in discovering the answers that will enable us to engage in God's mission more faithfully.

Perspective Three: Role

The final insight I want to consider before moving on to specific leadership practices comes from Ronald Goleman, who has researched and written extensively in the area of emotional intelligence. In the book *Primal Leadership: Realizing the Power of Emotional Intelligence*, written with Richard Boyatzis and Annie McKeem, he describes six distinctive leadership styles.[20] They are:

- visionary—articulating shared dreams for the future
- coaching—connecting personal and organizational goals
- affiliative—creating harmony through building relationships
- democratic—enhancing participation in decision-making

- pacesetting—showing the way to do it
- commanding—providing clear and detailed direction for others to follow

Goleman calls these styles the "leadership repertoire" and asserts that all of them have positive potential. While each of us may naturally prefer to use one of these styles, the needs of the people and organization we are leading may require us at times to use others.

These leadership styles emerged in a study of business leaders Goleman conducted. The book describes how they function in a corporate setting. The styles are, however, easily transferable to the congregation. In subsequent chapters we will explore specific uses of the styles. At this point let's look briefly at the context in which each of them can be effective.

The visionary style, Goleman's study demonstrated, is typically the most effective of all the styles, if the setting is right for it. Its aim is to articulate a guiding purpose for the organization that will allow participants to determine how they can contribute to the fulfillment of the purpose. Visionary leadership requires a level of trust in the leader and significant empathy on the part of the leader. Without empathy it is impossible for the leader to articulate a vision that resonates with the people. Without trust there is no reason for people to believe in the vision the leader articulates. The visionary style, because the leader articulates a vision and leaves the details to be worked out by others, also requires a relatively high level of commitment and participation from everyone. This style is particularly useful in congregations that are seeking to move into new areas of ministry or are committed to renewal and transformation.

The coaching style bears similarities to what is called "discipling" in some traditions. Traditionally, discipling has involved individuals spending time with new Christians to introduce them to the faith. It is a way the individual can learn about and adopt the beliefs and practices of the congregation. The coaching style is similar in that it aids individuals in their personal development in a way that connects with the purpose of the organization. It extends far beyond traditional discipling, however. Church members, for example, are coached to be more faithful and effective disciples, both within the congregation and in their communities. This coaching might include discovering spiritual gifts, discerning God's call to mission, or considering relationships from a faith perspective. At times it might be used to nurture leaders for the congregation. More often, however, it can be used to encourage an individual's involvement in home, work, and community as a person of faith. Since the coaching style seeks to improve performance, and since all of us seek to grow in our ability to live the life of faith, it is always important. If it is relied on exclusively, however, the leader can become exhausted, because there are always more people than any one person can coach.

The affiliative style builds a sense of community by enhancing relationships and focusing on those aspects of the congregation's life that create harmony. The affiliative style promotes the open sharing of emotions. The leader models this sharing and encourages it among all members of the organization. This style is particularly important during times when stress and uncertainty tend to overwhelm a congregation and undercut its ability to engage in ministry and mission. In the classic model of group life that involves both task and maintenance functions, this style focuses on maintenance, attending to the emotional needs of both individuals and the congregation. The focus on building a sense of community can lead, however, to an avoidance of those issues that might disrupt or disturb the warm feelings that the affiliative style seeks to develop. The leader needs to avoid falling into the head-in-the-sand syndrome that keeps any tension from being acknowledged. For that reason this style is most effective when used along with another style that focuses on task issues.

The *democratic style* is, in the free-church tradition, assumed to be primary. Free-church polity is, after all, modeled on democratic political practice. In North America the influence of the democratic political practice is felt even in churches that have a more hierarchical structure. This style does build the broad commitment of participants through involvement, but in some cases it can also work to ensure that nothing is done, because the consensus within an organization is never broad enough. The democratic style, however, involves something more than taking votes on every decision. In its broader sense it involves people in the process of making decisions. It works best in situations when direction is not clear and open discussion is needed to discover it. This style is therefore highly compatible with what Heifetz calls "giving the problem back to the people."

Leaders need to exercise caution in using the pacesetting and commanding styles. If used inappropriately or for too long a period of time, they can have a detrimental impact. *The pacesetting style* can be effective in raising standards and demonstrating new ways of doing things. If it is used excessively, however, it easily leads to resentment toward the leader and eventual burnout, as people are always being pushed to accomplish more. *The commanding style* has its place in crisis situations, when clear and decisive leadership is essential. Over the long run, however, people do not like being told what to do, so using this style can have considerable negative consequences. It may work well in the day or two after the church building burns down, but it is not a leadership style to use on a regular basis.

One challenge for leaders is to learn to use the style the situation requires. I have a natural bent toward the visionary and democratic styles. Most often I operate out of them and in doing so provide effective leadership. At times, however, the situation demands a more directive style. Sometimes the challenge we face is a new one, and the congregation doesn't have an appropriate response in its repertoire. The members need to hear, "Let's do this!" or see a way of responding modeled so that they can emulate it. I need to recognize such situations and be willing to move out of my comfort zone to provide leadership. I can usually return to my preferred styles before long, but I always need to remember that sometimes I will need to depart from them.

A Final Word about Relationships

Leadership is always about relationships. That truth underlies all three perspectives we've looked at in this chapter and will continue to be the unspoken assumption throughout the remainder of the book. I always assume that the nurture of positive relationships is a primary concern for leaders.

That's not always an easy thing. We'd prefer to avoid people who drive us up the wall. We may disagree with some members so often that it is difficult to be with them. Some have questionable motives. In these situations it can be difficult to work continually to develop positive relationships.

Here's a quick look at some of the reasons relationship is central to leadership:

How people *feel* about you is just as important as what they *think* about you, especially when it comes to their deciding whether to follow you. Relationships are the context in which feelings are developed. This is especially true within a congregation, which as a community puts a high premium on relationships and as a community of *faith* recognizes that it is about something more that thoughts and ideas. "Even if they get everything else just right, if leaders fail in this primal task of driving emotions in the right direction, nothing they do will work as well as it could or should."[21]

If people do not trust you, they have no reason to follow you. The only reason anyone chooses to trust you is that you have demonstrated a reliability and integrity in your relationship with him or her over time. Deep and intimate relationship isn't necessary (or even possible with everyone), but a relationship within which people come to know you, how you think and feel and act, and whether you can be depended upon is essential.

Change is especially painful for those who have much to lose. Usually these are the people who have been leaders in the congregation in earlier years, who have a vested interest in the status quo. If change is needed in a congregation, your relationship with those who resist that change may be all they can count on. If your relationship with them is strong, you can continue to offer that to them as assurance in the midst of change. If you have no relationship with them at all, there may be nothing left for them. "For opponents [of change] to turn around will cost them dearly. . . . For that reason, your opponents deserve more of your attention, as a matter of compassion, as well as a tactic of strategy and survival."[22]

An ongoing relationship with those who resist your leadership is also a key to learning what you need to know to lead effectively. Your relationship with them provides the context in which you can listen intently to understand the reasons for their resistance. "If it is crucial to know where people are at, then the people most critical to understand are those likely to be most upset by your agenda."[23]

Those are some of the practical reasons that relationships are important in the view of those who study businesses. We in the church also have theological reasons for affirming the importance of relationships. The very nature of the Trinity itself is relational. The community that is the body of Christ is based in relationships. It is in and through Jesus's relationships with his disciples and with those in need of his ministry that they (and we) discover the truth of John's proclamation that the Word became flesh and dwelt among us. The pastoral role itself is based in relationship. As leaders we need at times to test those relationships, perhaps even beyond the breaking point, to do what needs to be done. But the pastoral role always demands genuine and caring relationship.

In this chapter we've explored three perspectives on leadership. It is about servanthood. It is about change. It is about styles. And we've also affirmed the core truth that it is always about relationships. In the next chapters we will explore a number of key leadership practices and discover how each of these perspectives shapes the way we can enhance our practice of ministry.

CHAPTER 3

Attending to Self

Self-care is usually an afterthought—even in books. After the author deals with everything we need to be and do as leaders, there's a chapter reminding us that we should take time to care for ourselves—as if it's something that can fit into the free time left in the daily schedule. In an effort to break that pattern and establish self-care as a priority, we'll address this concern first. There is a danger putting self-care first, of course. It can appear (and sometimes become) self-centered and even selfish. It can lead to obsessive navel gazing, turning us inward when our call is to serve others. It can be used as a rationalization to avoid difficult challenges. Despite the dangers, however, it is a good place to begin. Without giving attention to ourselves, we end up being of little use to anyone else.

Self-care is the central factor nurturing the heart to develop the "who" of leadership. It is only when we attend to ourselves that our personhood emerges with authenticity. Time away from the demands of work, time to engage other interests, and time to do nothing are all essential. Self-care, as we will consider it, however, is more than taking time for ourselves. Genuine self-care also encompasses not just time away, but also deliberate attention to our continuing growth as people and as disciples. Our own personal growth has implications for our work, of course, and in that sense might not be strictly considered self-care. However, the continuing development of our own personhood leads us to deeper self-realization and personal fulfillment. And that is certainly self-care.

Why is giving significant attention to ourselves important? Yes, it's a way to avoid burnout. Yes, it's a way to prepare ourselves to serve others more effectively. Most important, however, it is the way we attend to one of the primary tasks and challenges of our lives: becoming the people God created us to be. We are created and gifted by God for a purpose. That purpose is to participate in God's mission of redeeming all creation. Even the best of us can manage only a very small part of all creation, but all of us have a responsibility to do what we can in the time and place that is ours. It's not just a responsibility, however—at least not in the sense of something that is laid on us that we are obligated to do no matter what. It is, rather, the fulfillment of our purpose in life. As we develop the gifts God has given us and respond to God's call to involvement in God's work in the world, we are living out the reason we are here—and this is the best and greatest source of our personal fulfillment. This involvement is impossible without careful, deliberate, and continuing attention to ourselves. Self-care is an integral part of the pilgrimage of life and faith that leads us to be more nearly the people God created us to be. In their book *The Spiritual Leader's Guide to Self-Care,* Lutheran pastors Rochelle Melander and Harold Eppley put it this way: "Self-care means living the life God has intended for you. You are God's own creation. Your task is to be yourself, the person God has called you to be. This includes creating a vision for your life and then crafting a life that honors that vision. It includes caring for your body, mind, spirit, and the resources God has given to you."[1]

We're all aware of the model Jesus provides for us, but it is worth repeating as we begin our look at self-care. The accounts of Jesus in the gospels demonstrate a clear pattern of engagement and retreat, time with others and time for himself and God. Before his ministry began, he spent forty days in the wilderness attending to his own growth and development, defining who he was and what his ministry would be. During his active ministry there were times of teaching and healing, but there were also times away to pray, both alone and with his closest disciples (Matt. 14:23, 19:13, 26:36; Luke 6:12, 19:28). Jesus found time for self-care, especially when he knew big decisions and tough times lay ahead. It would, I imagine, have been easy to develop a compelling rationale for constant engagement in ministry. After all, the results of Jesus's ministry were evident to all—much clearer than most of our own efforts. Jesus healed those who were sick; he cast out demons and gave sight to the blind; he commanded the lame to walk. Imagine what it must have taken for Jesus in effect to say to himself, "Today people will not be healed, demons will not be cast out, the blind won't recover their sight, and the lame will not begin to walk, because I need some self-care." It sounds a bit crass, doesn't it? But it does describe the impact of his decision to disengage from ministry and to attend to himself and his relationship with God. And it certainly makes a clear statement about the importance of this kind of disengaging for our own ministries!

Insights from the Theories

This need for self-care is something all leaders face, as is evident in the writing of secular theorists. While in many cases framed quite differently from a faith-oriented focus on self-care, these writings underscore the importance of self-care for anyone in a leadership position. It is simply not possible to lead effectively without attention to our own personhood, reflection on our own lives, and mindfulness about our own growth.

In *Leadership on the Line: Staying Alive through the Dangers of Leading,* Ronald Heifetz and Marty Linsky of the Kennedy School of Government at Harvard University devote significant attention to personal growth and development. In a section titled "Body and Soul," they talk about the need to manage our hungers and anchor ourselves. "Sometimes," they write, "we bring ourselves down by forgetting to pay attention to ourselves. We get caught up in the cause and forget that exercising leadership is, at heart, a personal activity."[2] Without giving attention to self-care we do harm, not only to ourselves, but also to others, our ministry, and the congregation. "Every human being needs some degree of power and control, affirmation and importance, as well as intimacy and delight. . . . Yet, each of these normal human needs can get us into trouble when we lose the personal wisdom and discipline required to manage them productively and fulfill them appropriately."[3] If we do not have a handle on our need for power and control, we can easily shift into authoritarian leadership and forget that the basis of power granted to any leader is the expectation that he or she will provide a necessary service. If we depend too much on others' affirmation, we can become beholden to those who applaud our every move, and we may begin to direct our leading in a way to win approval rather than attend to needs. If we do not care for our need for intimacy in appropriate ways, we can be easily tempted to meet it in ways that corrupt the legitimacy of our leadership and do harm to others. One of the aims of self-care, then, is to attend to our needs in healthy ways.

To address these needs appropriately, Heifetz and Linsky recommend that we first acknowledge them and their legitimacy. Second, they encourage the development of transition rituals that help us differentiate between our public and private lives. Finally, they note the vital importance of attending to the intimate relationships of our lives. "Otherwise . . . the hunger spills over in destructive ways, or we abandon that aspect of our humanity altogether."[4]

Additional strategies that Heifetz and Linsky suggest to promote our personal well-being as leaders are

1. developing an ability to distinguish role from self (recognizing that both the praise and the criticism we receive as leaders is most often motivated by people's perception of the way in which we are playing our role)

2. nurturing significant relationships with confidants who are not involved in the organization for which we are providing leadership

3. finding a sanctuary—"a place of reflection and renewal, where you can listen to yourself away from the dance floor, and the blare of the music, where you can reaffirm your deeper sense of self and purpose"[5]

Management consultant Stephen R. Covey names balanced self-renewal as one of the habits in *Seven Habits of Highly Effective People*. It is, in his view, "the habit that makes all the others possible."[6] He calls it "sharpening the saw." Using sawing as an image for the work in which we are engaged, he says we need to take time out to sharpen the saw, or our efforts will eventually be in vain.

In a similar vein in a later book, *Principle-Centered Leadership*, Covey affirms that one of the characteristics of such leaders is that they "regularly exercise the four dimensions of the human personality: physical, mental, emotional, spiritual."[7] Physically, they have a program of regular exercise. Mentally, they read and write and are involved in creative problem solving. Emotionally, they seek to grow in empathy and in taking responsibility for their own lives. Spiritually, they engage in prayer, Scripture reading, meditation, and fasting. A balanced approach to self-renewal is essential. Keeping all these dimensions in balance may not be easy, because some are likely to come more easily for one person than for others. "I'm convinced," Covey writes, "that if a person will spend one hour a day on these basic exercises, he or she will improve the quality, productivity, and satisfaction of every hour of the day, including the depth and restfulness of sleep."[8] This is yet another affirmation of the need for self-care in the lives of leaders. Self-care is valuable in and of itself in that it enables our growth as persons. But it is also the means to more effective leadership.

In his essay "Education and Maturity," Robert Greenleaf focuses on the emergence of that which is uniquely us as the essence of self-care. In Christian terms, this is the nurturing of the person God created us to be. Without this nurturing, we are less able, less capable than we might be. As Greenleaf describes it: "Only as what is uniquely me emerges do I experience moments of true creativity; moments which, when deeply felt, temper the pain of long periods of frustration that are the common lot of most of us and give me the impulse and the courage to act constructively in the outside world."[9] Greenleaf suggests four major issues to be faced, each of which provides a perspective on the dimensions of self-care.

The first of these issues is "the consequences of stress and responsibility."[10] Stress and responsibility are two of the burdens of leadership. When we carry them over a long period of time, they tend to wear us down, and we become narrower in our thinking, less open to new possibility, more victims of circumstances seemingly beyond our control. When I found myself in a particularly difficult ministry situation, I used continuing education funds not to attend a workshop, but to meet regularly with a trained counselor who became my consultant. We didn't delve into deep parts of my psyche or attempt to analyze the various neuroses at work in the congregation. What we did was to explore possible ways I could act. The burden of stress had shut down my ability to be creative, to see possibilities. Self-care for me in that situation was to meet with someone who could help me see things I couldn't see.

The second issue of importance to Greenleaf is "the tension between the requirement to conform and the essential person."[11] Conformity, despite the bad name it may have, is essential. All institutions require it, for it provides the common ground upon which people stand, act, and relate to each other. To be a leader necessitates conforming to the standards and practices that are held by the organization and the people we seek to lead. And yet, if there is nothing but conformity, individual identity is lost. If there is nothing but conformity, the organization eventually dies because there is no divergence from the norm to stimulate new ways of thinking and being. The challenge of the leader is to live within this tension. That means, on the one hand, to conform when it is essential, but at the same time to recognize that conformity is "a completely external adjustment to the group norm of behavior in the interest of group cohesiveness and effectiveness."[12] On the other side of this tension is our awareness of the essential person we are, which allows us to not let the need to conform shape our identity, as well as to determine when within the organization we can assert that identity.

The third issue is "the struggle for significance—the complications of status, property, achievement."[13] The key here is to find our own significance apart from the external measures that so often define success and provide a sense of accomplishment. Every institutional structure has these external measures of success and achievement. The problem comes when we start thinking, "I need to do these things to prove that I'm successful." If that happens, then moving to a larger congregation, climbing the denominational hierarchy, preaching and teaching in important places, and writing best-selling books become the standards by which we judge ourselves. These external measures offer a great temptation that can be resisted only with careful attention to self, continuing reflection on our motivations, and ample time away from the fray.

Finally, Greenleaf offers the concept of *entheos* as a way to develop a process for "drawing forth one's uniqueness."[14] *Entheos*, as Greenleaf defines it, is the power activating one who is inspired. Without *entheos* our leadership is in danger of becoming misdirected, if not actually perverse, motivated by false claims and inspired by inappropriate aspirations. While there is no one way to nurture *entheos*, Greenleaf offers several indicators of its presence and growth. First, he rejects a series of misleading indicators: material success, social status, meeting others' expectations, relative peace and quiet, busyness. He then goes on to offer several indicators that real growth is taking place:

- a concurrent satisfaction and dissatisfaction with the status quo
- a growing sense of purpose
- changing patterns and depths of interests in which former ones disappear and new and deeper ones emerge
- greater willingness to be seen as the person you are
- increased consciousness about the good use of time
- a growing sense of achieving basic personal goals through work
- an emergence of unity pulling together various aspects of life
- a developing view of people in which all are seen "as beings to be trusted, believed in, and loved, and less as objects to be used, competed with, or judged"[15]

He concludes, "The ultimate test of *entheos*, however, is an *intuitive feeling of oneness, of wholeness, of rightness*; but not necessarily comfort or ease."[16] I take great assurance in his profound insight that all good leaders are reasonably disturbed!

While these insights of secular writers do not offer specific methods of self-care for congregational leaders, they do provide an understanding of why it is essential to effective leadership. We'll look now at some specific methods of self-care as we explore insights for practice.

Insights for Practice

The self-care of congregational leaders is an issue of great interest these days. Much that is helpful and valuable has been written about it. We can't review all the material in this setting. Instead we'll try to organize some of it in a fashion that provides helpful handles on the disciplines of self-care. In doing that we'll consider the importance of relenting, relaxing, relinquishing, reconnecting, renewing, refreshing, restocking, and reflecting. While we'll look at these individually so that we can gain an understanding of each of them, it will become apparent as the discussion develops that they are all interconnected, and each one leads to the others.

Relenting—Ending the Denial

Kirk Jones, pastor, theologian, and author, believes one of the most significant factors "that contributes to widespread ministerial overload [is] ministers who are in denial about the severity of pastoral stress and about its awful pain and negative consequences."[17]

There are countless rationales congregational leaders, especially clergy, use to deny our need for self-care and the detrimental impact its absence has on our lives, our families, and our congregations. We are doing the Lord's work, which must take priority over everything else. And if we are doing the Lord's work, Paul has made it clear that we can do all things through Christ who strengthens us, so there is no need for self-care. People rely on us to support them in the tragedies and pain of life; it would be selfish to attend to ourselves and neglect others in need; lots of people work just as hard as or harder than I do, so I have no right to complain. While perhaps noble-sounding, these rationales are in fact rationalizations that undercut our ministry and our ability to be genuine and effective leaders.

If we look behind the rationalizations, we will likely encounter any number of realities that are significantly less altruistic. We might learn that we are in fact caught up in our own ego needs, living out of our need to be needed. We might discover that we are addicted to the affirmation that comes to us because of our self-sacrificing dedication to others. Or that we simply lack the ability to trust anyone else to do anything well. Or that we lack the faith that the world (and our congregation) is in God's hands, not our own. For all of these reasons (and you can probably name any number of others), we find it impossible to set boundaries around our personhood. We respond to all needs that come our way. At all times we maintain a compassionate countenance that invites others to share their burdens with us. There is no escape.

What we fail to do in all of this is recognize that this denial is in reality a form of abuse. Unlike child abuse and sexual abuse, the abuse of ourselves, as Jones points out, is generally accepted and is often affirmed by those who marvel at our self-sacrifice. This affirmation is a lie, however. The truth is something else altogether. "Well-doing, devoid of proper self-care is, at best, doing well poorly. Exemplary care for others is rooted in vigilant self-care."[18]

The first task of self-care, then, is to relent, to give up the pretense. We need to face the illegitimacy of the denials of our own needs and the injurious impact those denials have had. This task begins with developing a new understanding of the theology of call and ministry. Alban Institute consultant Roy Oswald puts it this way: "I must reinterpret my call to a parish as primarily a call to serve God, not necessarily to serve people. My first call is to be a liberated, whole human being. My first responsibility to my congregation is to be a joyful, redeemed human being. This works only if ministry is viewed as a communal activity with people in mission."[19] We, and all members of the congregation, are called to serve God. All of us have responsibility for this mission, but it doesn't depend on any one of us, even those who have been ordained to "full-time Christian service." Our ability to participate faithfully in that mission depends upon our regularly taking ourselves out of service for scheduled maintenance, so that we can attend to our continuing growth as the people and disciples God created us to be.

Relaxing—Finding and Nurturing the Child Within

The fall months had not been an easy time for me. The stresses and strains of leading a congregation had continued to pile up. People seemed particularly negative and difficult. And I'm certain my family was thinking the same about me. Then my twelve-year-old son talked me into going with him to a video arcade. Tossing all caution to the wind, I decided that I would not obsessively count quarters that day but simply enjoy the time we had together. Enjoy ourselves we did! Air hockey, skee-ball, arcade games—on and on it went. But the thing that really got me was the two-seat racing machine. Ben and I each had a steering wheel and a car to drive in the race. We could race against each other, as well as additional cars. Quarter after quarter went down the slot as we laughed, cheered, and groaned our way through race after race. Sometimes he'd win; sometimes I would. But what a time we had! The image of us sitting there laughing together still has not left me—even after more than thirteen years. There was something special, very special, about that moment. There we were, father and son, simply having fun together.

Without even knowing it, Ben was teaching me a lesson that day: play is important. Playing together is important to deep relationships. Learning to play is important to learning to live. Play is important, not because it is a way to escape (which of course it is), but because it is a way to re-create. It is a way to relieve the heaviness of our burdens. It is a way to re-energize ourselves for the challenges we face. It is a way of life that puts being ahead of doing, enjoying ahead of accomplishing. Ben couldn't explain it that way; that is not the way a twelve-year-old thinks. But deep inside, something told him just how important playing was to his well-being and mine. He was wise about this—much wiser than I.

And so, another task of self-care is relaxing. It is the way we find and nurture the child that remains within us no matter how old we are. It is a lesson we need to keep on learning. More recently I've had to learn it yet again. We moved back to New England in 2005. I grew up here, but I hadn't lived here in more than thirty years. That means I had never lived in a place where every single Boston Red Sox game was on television. We moved into our new house, and I began my three half-time jobs in October. I loved every minute of it. I worked hard to establish myself in the church, to develop a distance learning program in the seminary, to teach stimulating and enriching courses to students. There wasn't a minute of it I didn't enjoy, and like the Energizer Bunny, I kept going and going and going. Along about March, I began to have more trouble sleeping, and my brain began to play some weird tricks on me. But I kept going—until Opening Day. Then, and for the rest of the baseball season, the priority became carving time out of my day to watch the Red Sox. Not surprisingly, a lot changed. I relaxed. I slept better. The brain tricks ceased. Once again, I learned the important lesson. And now I know that taking time away from the work that must be done is essential and produces significant benefits. And I will continue to do that— at least during baseball season!

Our means of relaxing might be playing with a child or watching baseball or fishing or going to the health club or riding a motorcycle. Whatever it is, we all need time to play, to be like a child. No checklists are needed here, no advice from the experts. Telling stories is enough. They appeal to the child in us.

Relinquishing—Saying No

Self-care involves setting boundaries. We do that by saying no. M. Shawn Copeland, a Roman Catholic laywoman and associate professor of theology at Marquette University, describes the need for saying no this way:

> Tough decisions and persistent effort are required of those who seek lives that are whole and holy. If we are to grow in faithful living, we need to renounce the things that choke off the fullness of life that God intended for us, and we must follow through on our commitments to pray, to be conscientious, and to be

in mutually supportive relations with other faithful persons. These acts take self-discipline. We must learn the practice of saying no to that which crowds God out and yes to a way of life that makes space for God.[20]

A confession: One of my colleagues pointed out to me, with only a little bit of a gleam in her eye, that in preparing to write this chapter I had sent her some basic thoughts by e-mail—on Thanksgiving Day! So perhaps I haven't yet mastered this self-care task of saying no and setting boundaries. It isn't easy.

Even in the most caring and compassionate congregations, the responsibility for setting the boundaries that create space for self-care is most often our own. We cannot rely on others to do it. We are much more aware of the pressures we face, more aware of the lack of boundaries. Usually if others (with the exception of our spouses) notice that we are working too hard or saying yes to too many things, we long ago passed the point of doing too much.

Just saying no is not enough, however. Sheer willpower will not do it. We need to set saying no in a context that makes it a realistic and continuing possibility. Again Shawn Copeland provides some insight: "In and of itself, 'just saying no' is never an adequate response, whether to drugs or to any other alterative that is immediately attractive but ultimately destructive. . . . In order for a no to be effective, it must be placed in the larger context of a life-affirming yes."[21]

The specific nature of the larger yes is likely to vary from person to person. It depends on what provides a powerful and motivating vision for your ministry. One possibility is the theology of ministry we looked at earlier. Remember Roy Oswald's words: "My first call is to be a liberated, whole human being. My first responsibility to my congregation is to be a joyful, redeemed human being."[22] If this is the larger yes of your understanding of ministry, then saying no to those things that negate the possibility of being a liberated, whole, joyful, redeemed human being becomes possible. You might also find your larger yes in Ron Heifetz's discussion of adaptive change that we looked at in chapter 2. Giving the problem back to the people requires that we say no with great consistency. Or perhaps the insight about *entheos* from Robert Greenleaf is what provides the larger yes for you. Several of his indicators of growth apply directly to this ability to say no. A growing sense of purpose enables us to focus our involvements. A greater willingness to be seen as the people we are makes us less beholden to the demands of others. Increased consciousness about the good use of time enables us to set aside those things that are not related to our growing sense of purpose and to live as the people we are. An emergence of unity pulls together various aspects of life.

A prerequisite of all of these growth indicators, however, is that we have done the work suggested in the task of relenting—that we have looked honestly at ourselves and our motivations, so that we can set aside those that keep us from being the leaders God has called us to be, the people God created us to be. If we have done that and have allowed ourselves to be claimed by a larger vision of ourselves and our ministry, then saying no becomes a real possibility.

Reconnecting—Nurturing Relationships

My experience with my son in the video arcade was about my learning to play, but it was also (perhaps even more significantly) about taking time to nurture family relationships. Part of self-care needs to be developing and attending to the rituals of family life. When we do that, we and our families both benefit. The relaxing task is one that lends itself to family time, but it's not the only one. We may need to do some relenting and end the denial about ways in which our families have been neglected as we attended to "the Lord's work." A good bit of the relinquishing we need to do may be in saying no to other things, so that there is time left for our families. Self-care cannot be just about ourselves. It also needs to include those who are closest to us, those whose lives we hold in special trust—a trust even greater than the one we hold for members of our congregation.

Stories abound of pastors who neglect their families for their work in the church. We don't need to hear them again. What we do need to affirm as we consider self-care is that nurturing positive relationships with spouse and children is essential to our own self-care. The family is our place of belonging and acceptance. For our own sake, we need to care for that place to ensure that it is there for us and able to serve that role for us. The other side of the coin, of course, is that being a spouse or parent is a call from God, just as our call to ministry is. That means that nurturing relationships within the family is just as much "the Lord's work" as caring for people in the congregation. It is part of what it means to be faithful.

Although I have used the word family here, my understanding of that is something more than the traditional mother-father-children model. Of course, that is what it is for many. But in the sense I use it here, family is composed of those people with whom we have relationships of commitment and intimacy that extend and grow over time. All these family situations require time and effort on our part. When we are able to say no and relinquish some of the busyness of our lives, here is where the newfound time can first be invested—because this is the area of our lives most likely to be taken for granted. Time spent here will give us something we can take with us everywhere.

My wife, Judy, and I bought our first house in 1978. We lived there for ten years, during which time both our sons, Chris and Ben, were born. Because of that, the house is full of important memories for us. One of these is about the driveway. It wasn't much. It wasn't paved, just covered with small stones less than an inch in diameter. While we lived there, I did a good bit of traveling. Once, when Chris was about three, we were all standing at the end of the driveway as I was getting ready to get into the car to go to the airport. As Judy and I were talking, Chris picked up one of the small stones and gave it to me. Without thinking too much about it, I stuck it in my coat pocket.

During the trip, however, every time I put my hand in that pocket, I felt the stone. And I would think about him, my family, and all they meant to me. Somehow, even miles away from home, I felt closer to them. I kept the stone in the coat pocket for as long as I had that job. When I traveled, it was always there. I would touch it, clutch it, remember my wife and sons, and somehow feel not quite so far away.

Now that stone sits on my dresser and serves another purpose. I've looked at it often during the past years as Chris went off to college, spent a year in China, and settled down into his first, and now his second job. The years since he gave me that stone have brought many changes, and many more changes lie ahead for us and our relationship. As the years pass, there are longer times of being apart. But there will always be the stone—a simple little thing that will help me remember. Seeing it, touching it will bring back memories of the day he gave it to me. It will lead me to reflect on all that has happened since that time. It will help me affirm the continuing richness of our relationship—all he has meant to me and I to him. It will encourage me in the hope that no matter what changes the coming years bring, the richness of our family bond will always be there and always mean as much to us as it did that day in the driveway.

That's what family is all about. That's why reconnecting is vital to our self-care.

Renewing—Engaging the Spirit

I lived a good bit of my adult life in the Philadelphia suburbs. While always maintaining my loyalty to the Red Sox, I developed a more than a passing interest in the exploits of two Philadelphia sports teams—the Phillies and the Eagles. Philadelphia sports fans are notorious for being somewhat less than gracious. They are, after all, the ones who booed Santa Claus at a December football game! Bill Lyons, a *Philadelphia Inquirer* sports columnist, commented on this unrelenting outpouring of derision by describing Philadelphia as the place where "the rolling seas of negativity crash against the rocks of cynicism."[23] I've remembered those words because there have been times when I believed they might also be aptly used to describe some churches.

Certainly not all churches are like that. In fact, most aren't. But there are still times when most of us feel as though the waves are about to overwhelm us and the rocks are about to smash us to bits. We will not survive these times unless we have attended to the self-care task of renewing, of engaging the spirit within us and the Spirit that both comforts and emboldens us.

Using the story of Jesus in the storm on the Sea of Galilee (Mark 4:35–41), Kirk Jones talks about our need to get to the back of the boat as Jesus did.

> The back of the boat is that place where we may go to remember who and whose we are. It is the place where roles and responsibilities are no longer the matters at hand. What matters most in the back of the boat is that we receive a refreshing of mind, body, and spirit. What matters in the back of the boat is that we are at peace with ourselves and with our God, regardless of life's circumstances. What matters in the back of the boat is that delight is found, not in what we produce, but in what we can, if only for a moment, open ourselves to receiving unconditionally.[24]

Fortunately, the Christian tradition is rich in ways to do this. The classic Christian disciplines offer various approaches to renewing ourselves through engaging our own spirit and the Holy Spirit. Richard Foster's *Celebration of Discipline* reintroduced Protestants to many of these disciplines and broadened our vision beyond prayer and Bible study. Other books on spiritual disciplines provide even further insight. In addition, there are countless resources available that can help us integrate these classic disciplines into our lives.

More recently attention has also been given to disciplines that are somewhat different. Dykstra and Bass's *Practicing Our Faith* offers insights into important disciplines such as honoring the body, household economics, testimony, and healing. These disciplines are also rooted in Christian tradition but until recently had not been clearly seen as ways in which we deepen and enrich our faith. This book helped me see important faith practices in my own life that I had not recognized before. For the first time in my ministry I have recently been part of a group of clergy that meets regularly. We gather at the same table in a local restaurant every Wednesday morning for breakfast. It's not an obligation, but almost all of us make it just about every week. We offer thanks for our meal each week, but beyond that there is no established ritual. We talk about our lives and faith. We share some of our struggles. Sometimes we decide to do things together. But there is in this time together a true sense of hospitality, of openness to each other and shared commitment to faith and ministry. This past semester I had a Wednesday morning class and was unable to join the group. I realized over the course of the semester that something important was missing in my life. These Wednesday morning breakfasts had become a faith practice that both sustains and shapes my ministry.

Renewal can happen through what we do in our own practice of disciplines that lead us into deeper relationship with God and with ourselves. We can develop daily, weekly, monthly, and yearly patterns of engagement that bring renewal to our spirits, because they enable us to be present with the Spirit. While we can learn much about these disciplines from books, careful attention to our own patterns of life and faith is likely to provide significant insight. For me, one pattern revolves around the two or three days each week I travel an hour by myself to the seminary campus. My life is decidedly different those days, and so is the way in which I engage the Spirit. Many times these trips become a way for me, in the image of Kirk Jones, to move to the back of the boat. So too the somewhat less-than-classic disciplines of "staring at the walls" or "walking along the beach." But for me, these have become part of the pattern of renewal in my life.

Another approach to this task of renewing might be to work with a spiritual director or counselor, someone who can be a companion in the walk of faith. We might also participate in communal disciplines that provide for renewing. Many Protestants have begun to adopt the practice of regular retreats in a monastery. In this time away from the regular patterns of life and ministry, a time of temporary involvement in a faith community, we can experience yet another dimension of God's renewing Spirit.

Those disciplines of renewal that are essential to some can be all but useless to others. It is important that we not berate ourselves for finding little use in many of the disciplines that have come down to us and that others find meaningful. It is, however, essential that we find and engage in those disciplines that renew our spirits by engaging the Spirit. And it is essential that we see them as disciplines—something that takes effort and needs to be maintained with regularity.

Refreshing—Invigorating the Body

I don't think that the adage about the body being the temple of the spirit has worked its way very far down into my psyche. Whatever the reason, there are many days that I don't think my body makes a very good temple! And yet . . .

Both Stephen Covey and Roy Oswald mention physical well-being as one of the essential dimensions of self-care. *Practicing our Faith* includes honoring the body. It's clear that stress manifests itself in a variety of physical ways and that in attending to the body we can also attend to the stress. The care of the body is essential to our well-being. Body-care is part of self-care.

Stephanie Paulsell of Harvard Divinity School, in her book *Honoring the Body*, reminds us that care for the body is grounded in the central affirmations of our faith.

> The convictions, wonderments, and hope that orient Christians to God and the world form the bedrock upon which the Christian practice of honoring the body is built. . . . God judged the creation good, and so everything God created, including bodies of all sorts, is good. . . . God was somehow fully present

in a particular human body that lived in a particular time and place, the body of Jesus of Nazareth. . . . Early Christian testimony that this body also lived again after death shapes a profound Christian hope that undergirds the practice of honoring the body.[25]

To refresh ourselves by invigorating the body requires that we attend to its care through our habits of eating and exercise, our sexual practices, our appearance, our treatment of illness and disease, and our rest. Care for our own bodies also opens up the possibility of letting others care for our bodies in ways that care for our souls. In *Let Your Life Speak* Parker Palmer writes about his experience of depression and an experience that touched him in this deep nothingness:

[A] friend named Bill . . . stopped by my home every afternoon, sat me down in a chair, knelt in front of me, removed my shoes and socks, and for half an hour simply massaged my feet. He found the one place in my body where I could still experience feeling—and feel somewhat reconnected with the human race.[26]

This is what it means to honor the body. This is why it is essential to caring for ourselves.

Restocking—Learning New Ways

Much of self-care is about the "who" of leadership, the development of the person God created us to be. *Restocking* begins with the "what" of leadership, although it, too, enhances the "who" of leadership. In restocking we are concerned about acquiring the knowledge and developing the skills we need to be effective and faithful leaders. It's about the "goods" and "commodities" we need for leadership. Just below the surface, however, restocking is also about self-care and the "who" of leadership. As we enhance our knowledge about and skills for addressing the challenges we face in ministry, we increase our effectiveness in dealing with those challenges. At the same time, however, we also develop the personal capacity that allows us to deal with the challenges without undue strain to our personhood. If we know more and can do more, the challenges of ministry take less out of us. When, for example, we increase our knowledge of the congregational system and our skills for dealing with the dynamics of that system, we not only function more effectively; we also function with less stress and strain.

Like most of the tasks of self-care, restocking can easily be taken too far, and its potential benefits destroyed. We can be so driven by a need to acquire knowledge and to develop skills that we have even less time for self-care. We can let this drive consume us, rather than use it to enhance us.

Part of our self-care should be the continuing development of ourselves through reading and continuing education. The skills needed for faithful ministry are constantly evolving in this rapidly changing world. We simply can't expect to have learned everything we need to know about ministry in kindergarten, or even seminary.

Reflecting—Increasing Self-Awareness

The film *Bull Durham* tells the story of Annie Savoy (Susan Sarandon) and her relationship with minor-league baseball players Crash Davis (Kevin Costner) and "Nuke" LaLoosh (Tim Robbins). Crash is the older, reflective player whose role on the team is to nurture the development of young pitchers, such as "Nuke," who thinks life is about little more than having sex and throwing a fastball. Toward the end of the season, "Nuke" is called up to the major-league team. In reflecting upon this harsh reality confronting Crash, Annie says, "The world is made for people who are not cursed with self-awareness." There are days I believe there is great truth in this comment. On my better days, however, I realize that reflecting in a way that increases our self-awareness is essential to faithful living and leading.

This reflection can happen in any number of ways. A number of self-assessment tools are available, as well as

inventories that need to be administered by trained profes-
sionals, that help us look at ourselves, our personalities,
and our leadership styles. These can be exceedingly helpful.
However, we ourselves can periodically take stock and assess
our growth.

When I was in my early thirties, I had the great fortune
to develop a relationship with Robert Greenleaf, whose
writing about servant leadership informs much of my own
understanding of leadership and whose insights are shared
throughout this book. In one of our discussions, I asked
him what I could do to enhance my effectiveness as a leader,
thinking primarily about the kinds of training events I might
attend. He replied by reflecting on his own growth, saying
that what he had found most helpful was following up the
various experiences of life by asking, "Now, what did I learn
from that?" This question has become the key to my own
reflection and self-assessment. My answer to that question
inevitably brings insight about what I might have done differently and what I should do next time. But it also brings
insight about who I am, how I react, and the ways I have
grown and still need to grow.

Moving beyond that single question, I have also found
that Greenleaf's tests of maturity, which I shared earlier in
this chapter, are an exceedingly helpful way for me to assess my growth. Every six months or so, I reread the essay
"Education and Maturity" and reflect on the ways I have or
have not managed to mature. His description of *entheos* has
been particularly helpful to me.

Norman Shawchuck, author and congregational consultant, also provides an interesting template that Christian
leaders can use in assessing themselves. "To remain true to
our call," he writes, "we must continuously examine our inner motivations and desires in the light of three attitudes that
Christ taught as the foundation blocks of all Christian leadership: to be as children, paupers, and servants before God
and the people."[27] As children we need to rely on God and
regularly engage in creative playfulness. As paupers we need

to guard against dependence on the riches of admiration, re-spect, adulation, prestige, and power. As servants we need to reflect in our leadership that which we see in God.

We've covered a lot of ground in our discussion of self-care. I hope the framework I've suggested will provide some helpful hooks upon which to hang our efforts at attending more carefully to ourselves. The other leadership practices we will explore in this book are much more public than self-care. If we falter in any one of them, that fact will be public knowledge. While it might not necessarily be talked about, it will be known. When it comes to self-care, however, we are dealing with a more private arena. We can (and often do) get away with neglecting this practice. Part of our challenge, then, in attending to self-care is to recognize this tendency and take the necessary steps to avoid it. We, our families, our congregations, and our ministry will all be better for it.

CHAPTER 4

Modeling Faithfulness

What does it mean to model faithfulness? The author of 1
Timothy had his ideas:

> Now a bishop must be above reproach, married only
> once, temperate, sensible, respectable, hospitable, an
> apt teacher, not a drunkard, not violent but gentle,
> not quarrelsome, and not a lover of money. He must
> manage his own household well, keeping his children
> submissive and respectful in every way—for if some-
> one does not know how to manage his own house-
> hold, how can he take care of God's church?
> —1 Timothy 3:2–5

While a number of these characteristics are certainly
worthy aspirations, it is also true that more than one pastor's family has suffered under the pressure of perfection
that seems to be implied here. I was once accosted by an an-
gry parishioner after a memorial service for a young mother
in which I had reflected on the way she and her husband
had shared with my wife and me about the challenges we
faced in raising young children. Clearly a biblical scholar,

the man glared at me and said simply, "1 Timothy 3:4."

This pressure for perfection has affected pastors and their families since the beginning of the church. The criteria may have been different in earlier times, but there has almost always been an ideal held out for the pastor to achieve. Pastors needed to drive a certain kind of car—not too nice and certainly not flashy! Pastors' wives should play the piano or teach Sunday school. Pastors must not be divorced. Pastors' children must be well-behaved at all times. Pastors must dress a certain way, talk a certain way, act a certain way. To violate any of these criteria would be to destroy credibility in the eyes of the congregation. In an interview I was asked by a member of a search committee how I would respond if a member of the church asked me to shave my mustache. Having already decided that this was not the right church for me, I told him I'd say I was sorry he didn't like it, but whether I had a mustache was really none of his business. Perhaps this is not an issue to stake a pastorate on, but it does illustrate the extent to which congregations can go in expecting a certain model of leadership.

These expectations have forced many pastors' families into all manner of deceit. I served as a pastor in a town where members of the police force were told to stop making drug busts in the local park, because they reflected badly on the community. This need to project an image has led more than one pastor to refuse to face problems within his or her own family, in the hope of maintaining respectability and credibility. It is impossible to live a lie forever. Unfortunately, however, it is possible to live one until it is too late.

These experiences speak to the danger of talking about the need for congregational leaders to model faithfulness. These images of perfection need to be set aside, as do the various behavioral expectations congregations have of their leaders. They do need to be taken seriously and dealt with in one way or another, because they shape relationships within a congregation. But they are not what we are concerned with here. Modeling faithfulness for us is something altogether different.

Insights from the Theories

First, let me note that virtually all leadership theorists believe that modeling is essential to effective leadership. You simply cannot lead others if you do not put words into action in a way that demonstrates both where you are leading them and how you are going to lead. Here's a quick sampling:

"Leaders should be doing, and should be seen to be doing, that which they expect and require others to do."[1]

"Be the change you want to see."[2]

"The very essence of leadership [is] going out ahead to show the way. . . . A leader ventures to say, 'I will go; come with me!' A leader initiates, provides the ideas and the structure, and takes the risk of failure along with the chance of success. A leader says, 'I will go, follow me!' while knowing that the path is uncertain, even dangerous."[3]

"Eloquent speeches about common values, however, aren't nearly enough. Leaders' deeds are far more important than their words, when determining how serious they really are about what they say. Words and deeds must be consistent."[4]

Modeling Values

James M. Kouzes and Barry Z. Posner have written what many believe to be the definitive text on leadership in today's world. *The Leadership Challenge* is now in its fourth edition and has sold over a million and a half copies. The book is built around the description of five practices of exemplary leadership. The first one is "Model the Way." "Exemplary leaders know that if they want to gain commitment and achieve the highest standards, they must be models of the behavior they expect of others."[5] On the basis of extensive research Kouzes and Posner have defined two commitments they believe are essential for leaders seeking to develop this practice. First, leaders must define themselves by clarifying their own values and establishing the guiding principles of their leadership. This step is what establishes the leader's identity and lets others know who the leader is. Second, leaders must set the example by working to establish shared values and aligning their own actions with those values. The second commitment relates the leader to the broader purposes of those within the organization and provides a reason for others to follow by giving them confidence that their own goals will be furthered if they do.

While modeling the right behavior is a public act, its foundation is a personal one. Right modeling is possible only when values are both clear and deeply held. "The answer to the question of values will come only when you're willing to take a journey through your inner territory—a journey that'll require opening doors that are shut, walking in dark spaces that are frightening, and touching the flame that burns. But at the end is truth."[6] We will return to Kouzes and Posner's insights about shared values in the chapter on establishing common ground. For now, however, their insight that the ability to model effectively is based in our lived values is an important one to keep in mind.

Stephen R. Covey, author of *Principle-Centered Leadership*, understands character to be one of the six essential conditions of empowerment. It is, in his view, essential to the effective leader who empowers others in their work.[7] "Character is what a person is."[8] It is constantly revealed in what we say and how we act. The character modeled by the leader influences the lives of those who follow, as well as the organization in which they work. In this sense, character is a neutral word. We cannot help but model our character (who we are), no matter what it might be. For the principle-centered leader, however, the essential character traits are integrity, maturity, and the abundance mentality. Integrity seeks the congruence of values with habits, words with deeds, and expressions with feelings. Maturity is evidenced in courage balanced with consideration—the ability to strive for goals, while remaining aware of and sensitive to people. The abundance mentality is based in the conviction that "there is plenty out there for everybody"[9]—that our success does not depend on the failure of others.

Robert Greenleaf, whose work on servant leadership was discussed in chapter 2, also sees the modeling of values as essential to leadership. For him, the values that are foremost are those that demonstrate and promote genuine servanthood. By adhering to these values the leader demonstrates servanthood. This is also the way those who follow are more likely to become servants. In the introduction to *The Power of Servant Leadership*, a collection of Greenleaf's essays, Larry Spears, former CEO of the Greenleaf Center for Servant Leadership, summarizes the ten characteristics of the servant leader that emerge from Greenleaf's writings. These are, in essence, the values that the servant leader both espouses and lives by in his or her leadership: listening, empathy, healing, awareness (of the situation, of others and of self), persuasion (rather than coercion or manipulation), conceptualization (seeing things in the context of the big picture, the long-term possibilities), foresight, stewardship (a sense of holding all things in trust for others), commitment to the growth of people, and building community.[10] In Greenleaf's view, these values create the trust that is essential for followers to follow willingly. In living out these values, the leader develops trust but also provides the concrete example followers need to be servant leaders themselves.

Modeling Authenticity

We model authenticity by doing the thing we ask those who follow us to do. One aspect of this authenticity can be seen in Robert Quinn's discussion of the responsibility of the leader to model change. If all leadership is about change, as discussed in chapter 2, then modeling faithfulness as a leader is about modeling change. In Quinn's words, leading change requires "walking naked into the land of uncertainty."[11] Interesting modeling!

To lead change in an organization requires the ability to assess and define reality, to see the possibility of a new future, to mobilize support, to confront resistance, to provide encouragement. Change is a complex and difficult process

that requires great skill. And yet, without a personal modeling of change, without a confident and credible presence, all
the skill we can muster will go to waste. This is how Quinn
describes the need for the leader to model personal change:

> One key to successful leadership is continuous per-
> sonal change. Personal change is a reflection of our
> inner growth and empowerment. Empowered leaders
> are the only ones who can induce real change. They
> can forcefully communicate at a level beyond telling.
> By having the courage to change themselves, they
> model the behavior they are asking of others. Clearly
> understood by almost everyone, this message, based
> in integrity, is incredibly powerful. It builds trust and
> credibility and helps others confront the risk of em-
> powering themselves.[12]

To model personal change, leaders must resist the normal
responses to stress. In such times "there is a tendency to become rigid. Instead of responding creatively, when innovative
action is most needed, people increase their commitment to
their old patterns. They may implement their most ingrained
natural response."[13] This falling back into old, established
patterns is often very easy to see in others, but extremely difficult to see in ourselves. And yet, our own ability to avoid
old ways is the source of the credibility that enables us to
lead change.

Here's what it takes, says Quinn: "To thwart our de-
fense mechanisms and bypass slow death, we must confront
first our own hypocrisy and cowardice. We must recognize
the lies we have been telling ourselves. We must acknowledge
our own weakness, greed, insensitivity, and lack of vision
and courage."[14] Not an easy task! But here's where it leads:

> If we do so, we begin to understand the clear need for
> a course correction, and we slowly begin to reinvent
> our self. The transition is painful, and we are often

hesitant, fearing that we lack the courage and confidence to proceed. We uncover a great paradoxical
truth. Change is hell. Yet not to change, to stay on
the path of slow death, is also hell. The difference is
that the hell of deep change . . . puts us on the path of
exhilaration, growth, and progress.[15]

This is what such modeling is all about: "The fact that we
have enough trust and belief in ourselves to pursue our vision
is what signals to others that the vision is worth investing
in. Our message is filled with integrity and good intentions.
However, it is usually our actions, not our words, that send
the message."[16]

In the imagery we considered in chapter 1, the "who"
and the "what" of leadership are intimately connected when
it comes to modeling. It is a matter of both heart and mind.
We cannot simply "act" the part. The "who" and the "what"
must be aligned with each other if there is to be credibility.
We cannot but show who we are in and through our leadership. We may have the essential skills and knowledge that the
"what" of leadership requires, but if we do not model in our
own lives both the goal and the purpose of our leadership,
we will end up with few genuine followers. Secular theorists
are clear about this necessity. When, however, we move to
the realm of faith, where our goal is nothing less than the
kingdom of God and our way nothing less than that of Jesus,
modeling moves to an entirely different plane.

Insights for Practice

It takes a certain degree of arrogance even to talk about being models of faithfulness. Perhaps we might try to be models of attempted faithfulness or models of taking faithfulness
seriously, but realistically none of us can be a model of faithfulness. Not even Jesus's disciples could make that claim, for
time and time again, especially in Mark's Gospel, they proved

that they just did not get it. Jesus talked about the need for the Messiah to suffer and die, and Peter rebuked him (Mark 8:31–33). Jesus said the Son of Man would be betrayed and killed, and the disciples argued about who among them was the greatest (Mark 9:30–37). Jesus said that in Jerusalem he would be handed over and condemned to death but would rise on the third day, and James and John requested that they sit beside him in the kingdom and promised to share his fate, and the other disciples became jealous (Mark 10:32–45). Not only did they fail to model faithfulness; they consistently demonstrated that they didn't understand what faithfulness was all about. Even Jesus wasn't ready to make a claim of faithfulness for himself. "No one is good—except God alone," he said (Mark 10:18). If Jesus wasn't ready to claim goodness (let alone faithfulness), my guess is that we'd better be pretty careful when we talk about ourselves as models.

This isn't reason to give up before we begin, however. It is rather an essential caution that we must enter into this discussion of modeling faithfulness with a great deal of humility. It is reason for us to affirm that faithfulness is something other than perfection—that being faithful is not so much about living sinlessly as it is facing and confessing our sins and receiving forgiveness for them. The writer of 1 John has it right when he speaks of walking in the light: "If we say we have no sin, we deceive ourselves, and the truth is not in us" (1 John 1:8).

It is true that all of us have fallen short and are in need of forgiveness. It's also true that it is politically dangerous and theologically suspect to set up a hierarchy of virtue in which leaders, particularly clergy, are somehow either called by God to be, or in fact are, more virtuous than other Christians. And yet, we do expect more of our leaders. And it is probably right to do so. William H. Willimon, former dean of the chapel at Duke University and now United Methodist bishop for northern Alabama, puts it this way:

> The congregation is quite right in expecting that we are at least attempting, to a greater or lesser degree,

to embody the faith that we proclaim. The Christian faith is inherently performative, meant to be embodied, enacted in the world. To speak of the gospel skillfully without attempting to perform the gospel is a false proclamation of the gospel.[17]

If, then, there is some special obligation for clergy and other leaders to embody the gospel in their leadership, what is the reason for that, and what is the nature of the obligation?

Why Is Modeling Important?

Living a good, upright, moral life that is reflective of the gospel is, of course, important in and of itself. It is the right thing to do—the thing all Christians are called to do. Since our purpose is to consider the practicalities of leadership, we'll take a results-oriented approach to our discussion of the importance of modeling faithfulness. We'll look at what this modeling accomplishes with the organization and for the people we lead.

Modeling is important because it offers a picture of the way things can be. Modeling values is the central concern here. The secular writers we discussed earlier have this one right. By living the values of the vision that motivates us, we provide a picture of what we are striving to achieve.

That picture in many ways provides something similar to the proleptic presence of the kingdom in Jesus's ministry. The kingdom has not yet come, but it is already among us. As we live out of the values that will shape the future, that future becomes real even though it has not yet arrived. It is already but not yet with us. The "already" part, however, provides concrete evidence of the possibility that lies before us. It provides the motivation needed to start the journey and to endure the hardships along the way.

In our congregations, if our vision is of a community of caring, then we model caring. If it is of a community of truth, then we model truth telling. If it is of a community that reaches out to people on the margins of society, then we model reaching out and serving others. If it is of a community of spiritual depth, then we model the practice of spiritual disciplines. In the next chapter we will talk about vision. Some people need to act their way into a vision; they cannot develop one in the abstract. Modeling values is one of the ways we make acting into a vision possible. Leaders provide the example of what life will be like when the vision becomes real. When others catch the glimpse of possibility that modeling provides, they are more likely to follow.

I struggled quite a while to move one of the congregations I served out of its usual, customary, and rather formal ways of doing things. The members simply did not want to take the risk of doing anything differently. I fumed and fretted over their inability to loosen up until one day I realized I was the one who needed to change first. I was the one who needed to loosen up and take the risk of doing something different. The beginning point for me was giving up my sermon manuscript and getting out of the pulpit when I preached. That was hard for me to do. I lost something important to me when my preaching was no longer based in the carefully crafted phrases and thoughtfully composed allusions that were possible when I wrote a manuscript. But I gave up the manuscript, moved to the central aisle of the sanctuary, and started preaching in a whole new way. No great change. Certainly not the kind of deep change Robert Quinn talks about. I definitely wasn't "walking naked into the land of uncertainty," but I was modeling something I had been talking about, demonstrating the value I had been espousing.

Modeling is important because it is the way a leader creates trust. Modeling authenticity is central here. People will not follow someone whom they do not trust. Trust is the only basis for taking the risk of doing things differently. It is the only thing that keeps people going when the harsher realities of change begin to emerge. Trust is based in authenticity—in the faith that a person *is* who she says she is, *will do* what he says he will do. Even more, authenticity is based in the belief that, at least to some extent, the person has already done what she is asking others to do—and has survived. Earlier in this chapter Robert Quinn offered a perspective on this kind of authenticity based in his belief that deep change is the primary leadership task. The same need for authenticity applies to other dimensions of leadership. For example, Norman Shawchuck and Roger Hueser, authors of *Leading Congregations*, see the need for it to encourage spiritual growth in a congregation. "The most important thing a pastor brings to the spirituality of the congregation is his or her own experience and example. There is much that can and should be taught about spirituality; nonetheless the congregation will never understand or desire the spiritual journey proffered by the Spirit until they see and feel it in the experience and example of their pastors."[18]

Certainly the values of caring and confidentiality are also essential in building trust. People will not follow those who do not exhibit genuine care for them and their well-being or who abuse the trust that has been placed in them. As important as these qualities are, however, they cannot take the place of the authentic experience of the leader in building a trust that enables others to follow willingly.

The church I now serve faces an uncertain future. As deeply caring and committed as the people are, financial realities are forcing us to ask searching questions about our future and what God is calling us to be and to do. This venture into the unknown is difficult for all of us. Part of what keeps us going, however, is the experience I have to offer to the congregation. In recent years I've had to contend with the sudden loss of a job and income. In that time of waiting for something new to emerge, my mantra was "God is up to something." Over time I discovered that part of what God was up to was bringing me to this congregation as its pastor. Telling that story has provided an authenticity to my leadership amid great uncertainty—authenticity that I could not have gained had I not experienced and survived the kind of upheaval that may lie ahead for the congregation. Already the refrain "God is up to something" is beginning to shape our approach to the challenges we face.

What Is It We Model When We Model Faithfulness?

When we model faithfulness we model kingdom values and kingdom ways.

We could create extensive lists of those kingdom values. We see them in the Beatitudes and throughout the Sermon on the Mount (Matt. 5:1–7:28)—poor in spirit, meek, merciful, pure in heart. We see them in Paul's discussion of the fruit of the Spirit (Gal. 5:22)—love, joy, peace, patience, kindness, generosity, faithfulness, gentleness, and self-control. We see them in the ministry of Jesus—compassion, love, humility, confidence, giving, risking, sacrificing. All of these are values that provide insight into the kingdom that is already but not yet with us. Our modeling of them brings the reality of the kingdom closer, enabling others to gain a better sense of what it is and why it is the course of full and abundant life, both for them and for others.

None of us can do it all. The insight that Kouzes and Posner provided earlier in this chapter is important here. There is a sense in which each of us must define our own values. For the Christian leader this self-definition takes place within the context provided by the values of the kingdom. We cannot approach our selection of values as if we had a grab bag out of which to pick whatever values happen to appeal to us. It is up to us, however, to focus our efforts on those values that are most clearly an expression of the people God created us to be and the vision that God has for the community that we serve.

Modeling faithfulness is more than living kingdom values, however. It is also about living in kingdom ways. Faithfulness is making the journey of faith with honesty and integrity. It is acknowledging the struggles and the failures. It is confessing our sin and receiving God's forgiveness and the forgiveness of those we have harmed. While the standards for the leader may be high, we model faithfulness, not perfection. Part of being faithful is to acknowledge that there are times we do fall short, we do struggle, we are uncertain.

The Psalms provide an important insight for us. They are models of what it means to be faithful. Part of it is offering praise and thanksgiving to God (Ps. 95). Part of it is taking "delight in the law of the Lord" (Ps. 1). Part of it is trusting in the care of God (Ps. 121). And part of it is also challenging God when we feel forsaken (Ps. 22) and demanding a response from God when we feel ignored (Ps. 4) and humbly confessing our failures to God when we have sinned (Ps. 32).

The Psalms provide for us a model of honest and authentic faith. Our aim as leaders who model faithfulness is to bring the Psalms to life in who we are and in the way we live.

CHAPTER 5

Discerning Vision

Everyone knows that where there is no vision the people perish—everyone that is, except the author of Proverbs, who actually wrote, "Where there is no revelation, the people cast off restraint; but blessed is he who keeps the law" (Prov. 29:18). The proverb wasn't about a liberating vision of the future at all, but rather about understanding how to stay within the dictates of the law. Perhaps even a biblical mistranslation can capture an important truth, however! A compelling vision of the future is important for both individuals and organizations. For congregations it is essential, because God is always calling the church to be and to do more than it is right now. That doesn't mean "more" in the sense of busyness. It's not a quantitative "more." It's a qualitative "more." Without a sense of what that "more" is, it's impossible to respond faithfully to God's call to be the church. That's where vision comes in.

We know that we need a vision, but it's not always easy to discover the right one for us. We could organize a vision community and develop an eloquent vision statement, adopt it by an overwhelming vote of the congregation, and print it each week in the bulletin; but that doesn't necessarily mean it will be a vision that challenges, motivates, and empowers for ministry. Sometimes a force is at work in a congregation that challenges, motivates, and empowers for ministry, and yet it is difficult to put into words.

Much has been written about the importance of vision—both for businesses and congregations. Depending on which author you read, a vision may shape the mission or follow from the mission; the statement of it must be no longer than two sentences, or it can be several pages in length; it must be written or can be "a song in the heart." In almost all cases, however, vision is a step in a strategic planning process that the congregation uses to determine its future. The truth is, it's all pretty confusing. To cut through that confusion, let's approach the issue of discerning and communicating vision in a slightly different way—drawing on the insights of others, but shaping those insights into an approach that honors the presence of God in the life of a congregation and recognizes the organic nature of congregational life. Before we begin that, however, let's look at four preliminary thoughts about vision.

First, the process of "visioning" presented by many sounds more complex than it needs to be. The vision process is nothing more than a conversation concerning what we are about as a church, how it's different from what happens elsewhere, and why it matters. It's a conversation in which a wide range of people participate, but one in which God also plays an essential role.

Second, vision is essential for a congregation, because without it the congregation's mission is overpowered by cultural models that are competitive, market-driven, and focused more on institutional maintenance and strength than on mission and servanthood. Our culture is so thoroughly infused with these models that if a congregation does not have a compelling alternative to shape what it does, it will without thought or effort fall into one of those models.

The *third* essential affirmation is that for the church, the vision is always God's. It is God's vision for the congregation that matters, not our own. The key issue for the congregation, then, is how God's vision is discerned. It's never about developing or crafting our own vision; it's always about attuning ourselves to God's vision for the congregation—what God wants us to be and do to be engaged in God's work in our time and place. This model is different from most secular approaches to vision; it makes clear why it is dangerous for congregations simply to pick up secular models and apply them. We'll be looking at some secular models a bit later, but always with this awareness of the radical difference. This approach also challenges the one taken by some authors who write about congregations. Often they have bought in to a secular model, adapted it somewhat for use in the congregation, but failed to recognize this essential and radical difference in perspective.

Fourth, the role of the pastor is critical. The role is not, however, as some would have it, to provide the vision for the congregation. More important, it is to provide a setting in which the congregation can discern God's vision. How the pastor does this will vary depending upon the context, but this is always the central and essential role of the pastor. It's not that the pastor is the only one who can or should do this. But if the pastor isn't willing or able to play this role, the process of discerning God's vision for a congregation is most likely doomed.

Insights from the Theories

As we noted earlier, just about everyone these days talks about the "vision thing." Nonetheless, there is no commonly accepted understanding of what a vision is—no definition we can use to ensure that we are all talking about the same thing. Understandings of visions are shaped by the effect they have on an organization. So rather than seek a clear and common definition of vision, we'll look at a number of affirmations about what it is, what it does, and where it comes from.

Vision: What It Is
A vision is a picture of the future. In *The Leadership Challenge* Kouzes and Posner define vision as "an ideal and unique

image of the future for the common good."[1] Another secular writer, Robert E. Quinn of the University of Michigan Business School, sees it as "the general framework of future direction."[2] For John Kotter, who teaches at Harvard Business School, vision is "a picture of the future with some implicit or explicit commentary on why people should strive to create that future."[3] Management consultant Peter Senge, author of *The Fifth Discipline*, adds yet another dimension: Vision "is not an idea. . . . It is, rather, a force in people's hearts, a force of impressive power. It may be inspired by an idea, but once it goes further—if it is compelling enough to acquire the support of more than one person—then it is no longer an abstraction. It is palpable."[4]

In *Leading Congregational Change,* church consultants Jim Herrington, Mike Bonem, and James Furr offer a faith-based perspective that echoes these basic understandings of vision. They set vision in the context of mission, which is a "general description of God's eternal purpose for the church."[5] In their view "mission provides the framework and boundaries for vision."[6] Within this context vision is "a clear, shared and compelling picture of the future to which God is calling the congregation."[7] Because it is clear, it is understood and followed. Because it is shared with others, it provides the basis for unity in purpose and direction. Because it is compelling, it motivates the congregation to action. Vision, as these authors use the term, originates with God, who gives it to the leaders of the congregation as they engage in an appropriate planning process.

Precise definitions may vary from writer to writer. For our purposes, however, it is enough to say that vision is a congregation's preferred picture of the future, a genuine expression of who the members want to be as the people of God, and more important, what God wants them to be.

The power of a vision of the future depends, however, upon its meaning for the present. So our next concern must be: what does vision do?

Vision: What It Does

Peter Senge echoes a number of leadership theorists in stressing the essential nature of vision for an organization. "Vision," he writes, "establishes the overarching goal." He goes on to say, "The loftiness of the target compels new ways of thinking and acting. A shared vision also provides a rudder to keep the learning process on course when stresses develop."[8] Or, as Kouzes and Posner put it, "The most important role of vision in organizational life is to give focus to human energy."[9] Vision, then, is a picture of the future that mobilizes and energizes the present. A vision of the future that does not shape the activity of the present has no value at all.

John Kotter describes three important purposes of a good vision:

1. It simplifies decision making by providing an overall direction.

2. It motivates action that supports the direction it articulates.

3. It coordinates the actions of the people who have claimed it.

To do these things the vision needs to be

- imaginable—so it can be grasped by others
- desirable—so people will want to be part of making it a reality
- feasible—so it can be accomplished
- focused—so it can provide direction for decision making
- flexible—so it can adjust to changing circumstances
- communicable—so it can be easily shared[10]

In their book, written specifically for congregations, Herrington, Bonem, and Furr draw on the insights of secular writers. For them vision "establishes an identity for the congregation—what we are, what we are not, and what we expect to become in three to five years."[11] Once the vision is established, it leads to a "visionpath" that shapes the work of the congregation.

What vision does, then, is to shape the work of the present. It focuses the congregation's attention and efforts on becoming something that the members want to be (or that they believe God is calling them to be). When the vision is clear, it is possible to determine what should and shouldn't be done. When the vision is powerful, it empowers members of the congregation to be about the work that will make it a reality. When a vision is articulated and shared, the congregation as a whole has a clearer sense of where it is going, and its members are more able to join the journey.

Let's be realistic, however. A vision can do great things for a congregation. But it doesn't, in and of itself, change everything. There will be those who want to continue the traditions of the past even if they are not compatible with the vision. There will be others who are devoted to having the building in pristine shape above all else, even if the vision focuses on using the building for ministry. There will be some whose priorities differ and who still believe this church, no matter what its vision may be, is still their church. Later we'll discuss practices that deal with the reality that everyone might not share the same vision for the congregation. For now, let's simply acknowledge that it is a truth of congregational life.

Vision: Where It Comes From

Before looking at understandings of how visions are developed, a few words are needed about why they are so difficult to come by. Robert Greenleaf, whose work on servant leadership we considered in chapter 2, provides some help here. Greenleaf asks, "Why are liberating visions so rare?" and offers two possible reasons. First, they are rare because society requires a high measure of stability. Without it, there would be chaos. "[T]hey are rare because a stable society requires that a powerful liberating vision must be difficult to deliver, and that the test for the benign character of such a vision shall be rigorous." He goes on to warn, "reformers take note: in the end, most people choose order—even if it is delivered to them by brutal nonservants."[12] Congregations, like society in general, need stability. In addition, one of the church's primary functions is the maintenance of a tradition. No wonder it is so difficult to develop a vision that is a powerful force for change in a congregation.

Greenleaf's second reason focuses not on society in general, but upon leadership. "So few of those who have the gift for summoning a vision, and the power to articulate it persuasively, have either the urge or the courage or the will to try!"[13] It seems a daunting task, and you could assume from these words that it is the sole responsibility of the leader to produce the vision. But it need not be a solitary endeavor. In Greenleaf's view, prophetic visions are not uncommon. What is uncommon is the capacity to hear them. Rather than being the visionary, then, it is possible that the leader will not be the one with a vision but "the convener, sustainer, discerning guide for seekers who wish to remain open to prophetic visions."[14] The key is to nurture the seekers in our midst.

Peter Senge builds on this notion of nurturing the seekers of visions. He sees an intimate connection between personal and corporate vision. An organization's vision is a by-product of individual visions. It's up to the organization to develop a context for conversation, to nurture the discussion about these visions, so that individual visions can be shared and a common corporate vision developed. The first step in the visioning process, in Senge's view, is "to give up traditional notions that visions are always announced from 'on-high' or come from the organization's institutionalized planning process."[15] Sometimes they do, but often they simply "bubble up" from the ongoing conversation about personal visions in an organization. These need to be conversations in which "individuals not only feel free to express their dreams, but learn how to listen to each others' dreams. Out of this listening, new insights into what is possible gradually emerge."[16]

In his book *Leading Change*, John Kotter discusses the development of vision within the context of a corporate change process. Although his focus is on the business world, his insights have had an appeal to many who work in nonprofit, educational, and religious settings. In Kotter's process, the steps prior to developing a vision are creating a sense of urgency (so that the need for change is clear) and nurturing trust within a guiding coalition (so that difficult issues can be addressed). Although he makes clear that the process cannot be rigid, his view is more compatible with a traditional institutional planning process than is Senge's, in that it is based in a linear process rather than in conversations. The vision-development process begins with a draft statement—most often written by an individual, usually the organization's primary leader. This statement is shared with a small group (the guiding coalition) and undergoes revision based on feedback from that group. This is often "a messy, difficult, and sometimes emotionally charged exercise,"[17] because it goes to the core of the organization's identity and purpose and often uncovers conflicting worldviews. It is only after a basic consensus emerges within this group that the vision statement is made public. But the vision is not set in stone at this point. Two-way communication is essential, as is openness to revision of the statement if the broader sharing brings new insights. Communicating the vision is just as important as developing it. Without a continuing commitment to this communication, the vision loses its power to shape the work of the organization.

In *Leading Congregational Change*, Herrington, Bonem, and Furr offer a faith-oriented twist on the work of secular writers. Although the process of organizational change they present resembles Kotter's in many aspects, they describe the process not as developing the organization's vision, but as discerning God's vision for the congregation.

> We . . . want to firmly and emphatically state that vision, as used in this book, originates from God. . . .

The Bible offers many stories of God implanting his vision in human leaders in order to accomplish his purposes. . . . Many of the church leaders with whom we have worked have clearly felt that God has given them a specific vision for their ministry and for their church, and has continued to confirm and shape that vision over time.[18]

They then offer a seven-step process of discernment:

1. Seek input—talking with others to learn more about the congregation.
2. Pray—to "acknowledge that God is at the center of the process and seek his guidance."
3. Write the first draft.
4. Seek private feedback—from a "trusted advisor."
5. Revise.
6. Obtain public feedback—at first from a previously established vision community and then more broadly.
7. Develop consensus.

This process is based in the following underlying beliefs:

*   Vision originates from God.
*   God empowers congregational leaders to discern the vision.
*   The senior pastor plays a central leadership role in the discernment and interpretation of this vision.
*   Involvement of a vision community can allow the pastor's vision to merge with the vision of individual lay leaders in a way that builds commitment to a shared vision.
*   The entire congregation must ultimately have the opportunity to shape and confirm the vision.[19]

Insights for Practice

At this point we have a fairly good picture of major issues related to vision. It's time to consider what these insights might mean for the practice of ministry in our own settings.

The insight provided by Herrington, Bonem, and Furr is a key to the practice of visioning in the congregation. The vision is not our own. It is God's vision for the congregation, what God is calling the congregation to be and do, that matters most and not what we want the congregation to be. That means we do not develop the vision; we discern it. To do that, we seek the guidance of the Holy Spirit.

As we do this, we need to be especially cautious of step-by-step, linear processes. These are tempting because they are straightforward and seemingly manageable. Unfortunately, the Holy Spirit refuses to be programmed and rarely does anything decently and in good order. There's always a bit of chaos involved—and there has been right from the Day of Pentecost. Strict adherence to a linear planning process can sap the life out of any organization. That is not to say, however, that a guiding spirit is not needed. For a leader, one way to offer guidance without adhering to a step-by-step process is to be aware of the steps of a process, but not to impose those steps on the congregation. It's important, for example, to know that gathering information, praying, testing out a possible vision with gradually larger groups, and revising the vision on the basis of feedback (all steps in the process described by Herrington and his colleagues) are important ingredients in the process of discerning a vision. In many if not most churches, however, it is not necessary (and may in fact be detrimental) to present these ingredients in the form of a deliberate process that the congregation must follow. The organic nature of most congregations demands a more fluid means of discerning vision than can be achieved by adherence to a step-by-step process. A linear process may produce a good bumper sticker or wall poster, but it doesn't usually transform a congregation.

The visioning process offered by Senge provides insight into another option. The key for Senge is creating the context for conversation. The leader seeks to establish a setting in which members of the congregation are encouraged to share their own visions. In a congregation, these can take two forms: (1) a vision for my own life and faith, and (2) a vision for the congregation. Again, the key here is developing the understanding that the vision comes from God, not the individual. So the important questions for the person to consider are: (1) What is God calling me to do? and (2) What is God calling this congregation to do? Neither of these questions can be answered in isolation. Both require open and honest conversation—conversation in which we trust that the Spirit is at work. As these conversations continue, they lead, as Senge suggests, to the development of a corporate vision. In the midst of these conversations, the various ingredients Herrington and his colleagues offer as steps in a process are present. There is information sharing, praying, drafting, and revising. But all of it happens more naturally, less mechanistically, because it happens in the context of conversation.[20]

I have been approaching the discernment of vision in the congregation I serve much more as a conversation than as a linear process. This approach fits the style of the congregation better than a formal planning process. The involvement is more honest; the results are more genuine. It takes much time to do things this way. And it's easy to get lost, because there is no map to follow. But I have a strong sense that the conversations encourage engagement with each other and with God's vision for the church that wouldn't happen otherwise. As I've been involved in this conversation, it has become clear that although I have never produced a written vision statement as such, my input as the pastor is significant. This is the way I see the role I have played.

It began with an understanding of the purpose of the church that I shared with the pastoral search committee in our initial conversations. For me, that purpose is to be a disciple-forming community—that is, a congregation that enables believers to develop an understanding of themselves as gifted and called by God for participation in God's work in the world, equips them, sends them into that ministry, and supports them while they do it.[21] Those conversations made clear that this sense of purpose resonated with the members of the committee, so I began work as their pastor knowing that I had shared the beginning of a vision with this group and that its members had responded positively to what I had to say. The task before me at that point was to share this sense of purpose more broadly, let the members of the congregation live it and live with it, and (assuming there was a broader resonance) let the vision for this church begin to emerge as we together thought and prayed and studied and acted our way into what it might mean to be a disciple-forming community. It was at this point that we began to commission members for various ministries as part of the worship service, so that we could recognize and support those who moved into the world with a sense of God's call. Rather than dedicate church school teachers, we commissioned them, offering our thanks and support for them in this ministry. We also commissioned members of the congregation who participate in the local homeless ministry. And when our church hosted the homeless for a week, we commissioned everyone who would be helping out in some way. We continued the conversation about vision through the development of our new church brochure, which gave us an opportunity to talk together about what it means to be what we say we are. But still, we are talking not so much about vision in all of this as purpose. We're trying to figure out what it means for us to live out our purpose. That will be our vision.

As we work on this task, I've discovered that I and others have shared what I'd call notions of what our church might become if it truly were a disciple-forming community. These are the seeds of our vision. In Senge's terms, these may be personal visions, but at this point they are probably not the corporate vision of the congregation. And we haven't had time to discern whether any of them are God's vision. I share my notions of what that vision might be like as others share theirs. This is how we engage in conversation and encourage the discernment process. We put some of the notions into practice, testing them to see if they really are what God wants us to do. And we ask a lot of questions: Might it be that for us to be a disciple-forming congregation, it's not necessary to have a building? Could we be a disciple-forming community without a paid pastor? For us to be a disciple-forming community, what kind of music would we sing? How does a disciple-forming community offer hospitality to the community in which it is located, especially to people who are on the margins? How can we possibly equip people for all the varied ministries to which they are called? It has been two years now, and we're just getting to the point where we may be ready to formalize the discerning by asking someone to work with us so that we can more clearly envision what God has in mind for us.

Now it's time for another dose of reality. We are doing these things—or at least something that looks pretty much like them. (I admit to embellishing a bit to make my point). We're also dealing with the mundane issues of keeping the building clean, balancing the budget, and trying to find a new pianist/organist/keyboardist/accompanist or anybody who will play something during our worship services. We still struggle with the desire to avoid conflict. And we still get impatient; we are often traumatized by what needs to be done, and sometimes we get on each others' nerves. The interesting thing for me, however, is that the further we get into this conversation, the more we see all the mundane tasks in a different light, and we see that they are related to this bigger issue of vision.

Tom Bandy, author and church consultant, says that a real vision is "a song in the heart." By that he means, I think, that it is something that lives within you, that it is about both music and lyrics (heart and mind). That is why it takes time to emerge. A whole body of people needs to be attuned to God. That is why prayer, Bible study, and other spiritual disciplines play the central role in discernment. The vision will come. It will emerge from the conversation. It may come in an individual who begins to sing the song. The key to determining if it is a valid vision is whether others join the singing. If they do, the vision is real.

For the conversation to be genuine it requires deep listening—listening beneath and beyond the words. Such attention requires respect for each other and a willingness to hear whatever is said. It might be helpful to develop guidelines for these conversations. A conversational covenant could list the qualities needed for such listening, such as listening without interrupting or judging, respecting differences of opinion, allowing everyone to speak, not dominating the discussion, and asking clarifying questions.

For the conversation to be helpful in discerning God's vision, people on the fringe of church life also need to be heard, for there may be profound insights in the reasons for their being on the periphery. One of the shortcomings of using current congregational leaders as the primary vision group is the omission of the clear voice of fringe members; without them, an essential dimension of the vision will be missing. Gathering meaningful input from fringe members requires more than sending out a survey or inviting anyone who would like to come to a meeting. It can happen only if the congregation takes the initiative to reach out to those on the fringe and makes it clear that their views will be honored and valued. In many congregations, leaders will need to overcome an almost automatic bias that those on the fringe are not as committed as those who are more fully involved, or that their faith isn't as deep. It will take openness to the real possibility that they are fringe members because the congregation falls short of God's vision and therefore does not provide what many people truly need from a church.

Those further out on the fringe also need to be part of this discernment process. People who do not attend any church can provide significant insight into what is missing in the church's ministry. They can help us shape a new understanding of the way in which the gospel can speak to them. "Lurking" isn't a traditional spiritual practice, but there is much to be gained by hanging out in public places—from coffee shops to park benches—and engaging in conversation with those who are there or simply listening to what they talk about.

Robert Quinn describes an organization as "a coalition of coalitions."[22] Within that coalition of coalitions, one coalition is usually dominant. It shapes the organization's identity, often not through public statements, but through the way in which its members act. Most dominant coalitions, because they are in control, find it difficult to see the need for change and even more difficult to do the things that bring about deep change. That is why attending to those on the fringe is so important. They are the ones who see the need for change; they are the ones who have the ability to help others see what they could not otherwise see, do what they could not otherwise do.

Because it is so difficult to see the need for change and the possibility of newness, people often need to live into a vision. They need to act it out before they can state it. Because this is true, it is often necessary to get people involved in new ministries before having an earnest and honest discussion about vision. Here is where the pastor can make a significant contribution by encouraging "deviant" behavior on the part of members. Anything that is different and has the potential to be a new expression of the gospel needs to be encouraged, recognized, affirmed, and protected. It might be using the church to house homeless men for a week or two during the winter. It might be using the piano instead of the organ in worship. It might be singing an inclusive-language doxology. It might be refusing to serve on a board, so that one has more time to be involved in mission and spiritual growth. None of these is earth shattering (at least in most congregations), but each of them has the potential to "rock the boat," which in turn causes people to think in new ways. None of these brings about quick change, but each of them can contribute to a climate in which the traditional ways of doing things are disrupted, so that people can begin to think in new ways about what God is calling them to be and do. There is a lot to be said for the deliberate disruption of usual and customary practice as we open ourselves to God's vision for the congregation.

Leadership Styles

We return now to Ronald Goleman's leadership repertoire to explore how discernment might be accomplished in settings that require various leadership styles. We will look at several of these to gain an understanding of the variety of approaches that are possible.

Discerning Vision as a Pacesetting Leader

Sometimes congregations find themselves mired in old, dysfunctional patterns of ministry. The focus has turned inward. The primary function has become institutional maintenance. And yet, there is a sense that something needs to change. Hard financial realities may suggest that the congregation has only a few more years before it will be forced to close. A sense of emptiness or stress or uncertainty may be present in the experience of people within the congregation. In such situations, it is often impossible for people to envision any other possibility. They have had no experience that offers a different way of doing things. They are so beaten down by their own experience that they see no possibility. They believe they are not capable of meeting the challenge that lies before them.

In this situation, it may be helpful for the pastoral leader to articulate her personal understanding of God's vision early in her ministry and to begin to live out that vision in what she does. She can do the things she believes the church members would be doing if they were living out of the vision. She can move out into the community in ministry, or invite new and different people to worship, or turn the discussion at board meetings away from maintenance to mission or to board members' own spiritual growth. In doing this she provides a picture of new possibilities and demonstrates that things can change. There is, however, a limit to how far this approach can go. It needs to be seen from the very beginning as a temporary approach. If it continues, it can easily lead to burnout, to overreliance on the pastor to do everything, to resentment against the pastor for changes that only she is involved in. To avoid these consequences, the pastor who takes this approach could, at the very beginning, set a definite timetable for withdrawal—a date at which she would begin to back off from doing everything she did initially. If people notice the changes (and perhaps begin to complain—or celebrate!), the result can be an openness in which conversation can happen about what the church is called to be. A better alternative, however, is to begin to involve more people in these new initiatives and to couple that step with the visioning conversations we discussed earlier.

Discerning Vision as a Coaching Leader

Sometimes a sense of urgency to be and do something different grows within a congregation. A new pastor may discover this situation at the beginning of a pastorate. Or a pastor may have been working for years to nurture a sense of urgency among the laity in the congregation. Whatever the source, it results in a strong and fairly widespread sense that something different needs to happen. In such a setting the pastor's role can be one of continuing to nurture the desire for change, encouraging and affirming people as they explore what that change might be, interpreting for them from a faith perspective what is going on so that they see God at work in it, and guiding the congregation through visioning conversations. Laity in both formal and informal leadership positions can also play a vital role in coaching the congregation as it discerns a clearer sense of God's vision.

Discerning Vision as a Democratic Leader

Sometimes the song in the heart is already being sung, and

a sense of God's vision is already present in a congregation. It just needs to be articulated in a way that brings broader awareness and commitment. In this situation a democratic leader can help guide an inclusive process of bringing into broader consciousness the sense of vision that is already present. Democratic process in the sense Goleman uses it is not a matter of taking a vote in which the majority wins. It is more about involving a wide spectrum of people in the decision-making process. In this case the visioning conversations are about helping the congregation discover what it already knows. No one, including the pastor, may be able to articulate it yet, but the vision is there, ready to be brought forth. The wide involvement of people in this discussion enhances both the awareness of and commitment to the vision that is claimed.

Discerning vision isn't easy. It takes time—even to be ready to begin. As I write this chapter, the congregation I serve has come to the realization that our ability to survive (and, we hope, thrive) depends upon our deciding what it is God wants us to be and do. It has taken a year of preliminary work to come to the point where we are beginning (at least in what we say) to be open to God's leading, being willing to change, to let go and follow God's lead. Even now, however, we need to move slowly. For it is one thing to talk about discernment and something else altogether to do it. We still need to become more practiced at listening, more comfortable with silence, more willing to live with the questions, more willing to trust our future to God. What we are beginning to understand, however, is that there is no other way for us.

CHAPTER 6

Creating and Sustaining
Common Ground

Creating common ground—it sounds simple enough. For a community to exist, its members need to have common ground upon which to stand—principles, values, a purpose, a hope, a vision for the future that they all affirm and that enables them to act together, even though there may be significant differences of opinion on other matters. In many congregations this common ground develops naturally. Newcomers stay because they find something (the worship, the Bible study group, the social-justice emphasis) that is important to them. Those who have been there for a long time have, at least in some way, helped shape that "something," so it is important to them, too. It *is* common ground. But this kind of common ground is not enough. All too often it proves to be little more than shifting sand. When winds blow and rains fall, the common ground is washed away.

This erosion is more often than not related to change. As I noted in chapter 2, all leadership is in one way or another about change. Even in more stable situations, the inability of an organism or community to change leads to slow death. In a time of rapid and radical change, the consequences of an inability to change are even more quickly and dramatically apparent. Given this reality, the common ground we as leaders in congregations are most interested in creating and sustaining is one that will remain even in the midst of significant change. This cannot be a least-common-denominator common ground that is nothing more than watered down platitudes with which no one could disagree. Neither can it be an only-those-who-agree-with-us-on-just-about-everything-can-be-here common ground that narrowly restricts freedom and creativity and makes any deviance from the norm impossible. It must be a common ground that allows for a healthy diversity of opinion, perspective, and experience. Since most significant change originates in differing opinions and values, diversity within the institution is essential if it continually seeks to adapt itself to the ever-changing environment. Without internal diversity, change will be delayed, usually until it is too late. Congregations need a common ground that encourages diversity and at the same time is based upon a strong sense of identity and purpose that brings unity.

A primary leadership practice, then, is to create and sustain common ground. A case can be made, of course, that God, not the leader, creates the common ground, since it is God who calls the church into being and gives its mission. So theologically, at least, the leadership role might not be creating common ground, but helping people to discover and affirm it. Even then, however, there is a role for human involvement and leadership in affirming common ground. Like the other practices we've considered, both art and skill, both heart and mind are involved in doing this. It is a matter of both what we as leaders know and who we as leaders are.

Values and vision are important factors in creating and sustaining common ground. We've discussed both of these in previous chapters, so here we will just offer a quick review of some important insights about them that relate to common ground. We'll then focus our attention on two additional factors: language and story.

Insights from the Theories

"The first responsibility of a leader is to define reality."[1] Those are the words with which Max DePree—former CEO of office furniture designer and manufacturer Herman Miller and author of books on leadership—begins his description of the leadership task. In this statement DePree provides a key insight into the way leaders create and sustain common ground. The reality that the leader defines (or, more accurately, takes the lead in defining) influences the way the congregation looks at itself, sees meaning in its life together, and determines its role in the world. This is the common ground upon which the organization stands.

Recapping Vision and Values

Vision can play a significant role in creating and sustaining common ground. It is, of course, not unrelated to the present reality of the organization, and yet it moves beyond that to present a future reality.

If a vision results from a process that involves the people of the organization and is an expression of their hoped-for future, it draws people together and unifies both their thinking and their deeds. For it to provide strong common ground, the vision needs to bubble up from below rather than be handed down from above. If it is handed down, it is likely, despite the leader's good intentions, to be narrower than it should be, because the leader's perspective is always a limited one; the leader cannot see what others in the organization can see. Additionally, a vision that is handed down most often does not generate broad-based support and commitment, because people have not had the opportunity to grapple with and shape it in a significant way. Only when the people in the organization are full participants in the process and have the ability to shape the vision is it possible to create solid common ground.

In chapter 4, "Modeling Faithfulness," we looked at Kouzes and Posner's insights on the importance of clarifying personal values in order to shape the guiding principles of the leader. Just as these personal values shape the leader, an organization's shared values shape its life together. As leaders work to identify and develop shared values, they strengthen common ground.

While vision provides the sense of what an organization wants to become, values offer an understanding of the way a group of people will work together as they seek to make that vision a reality. Once again, as with vision, there is both a present and future aspect to values. Current values influence an organization, and yet change is often linked to the establishment and practice of values that will be new to the organization. They may be stated values in the present reality, but the future vision calls for them to be actualized. Wesley Granberg-Michaelson, general secretary of the Reformed Church in America, describes the role of values in an organization this way:

> [M]ission and vision are not enough. As important as they are, they alone won't sustain the journey. Members of an organization also need to be clear about the values they will take with them to shape their culture and life, for people go more easily to somewhere new if they know that values and ways of behavior that they respect will be upheld and even strengthened.[2]

Shared values provide guidance for the way people will treat each other as they move through the changes needed to realize the vision for the future. They offer an affirmation of what the organization will take into that future, even though many things may change.

And yet, as with vision, values can also be seen as something we are growing into. They can be a statement of intention that recognizes we haven't yet made it. Margaret Wheatley, author and leadership consultant, talks about this role of value statements:

> Behaviors don't change just by announcing new values. We move only gradually into being able to act

congruently with those values. To do this, we have to develop much greater awareness of how we're acting: we have to become far more self-reflective than normal. And we have to help one another notice when we fall back into old behaviors. We will all slip back into the past—that is unavoidable—but when this happens, we agree to counsel one another with a generous spirit. Little by little, tested by events and crises, we learn how to enact these new values. We develop different patterns of behavior. We slowly become who we said we wanted to be.[3]

Leaders bear the major responsibility for creating a setting in which it is possible to have greater awareness of our actions, be more self-reflective, help others notice old behaviors, and counsel one another with a generous spirit. In doing this leaders help to build the common ground in an organization.

Shared values offer a basis for common ground if they are both owned and embodied by the members of the organization. Ownership comes through participation in the process of articulating the values. Kouzes and Posner observe:

Leaders must engage their constituents in a dialogue about values. A common understanding of values comes about through that dialogue; it emerges from a *process*, not a pronouncement. . . . Shared values are the result of listening, appreciating, building consensus, and practicing conflict resolution. For people to understand the values and come to agree with them, they must participate in the process: *unity is forged, not forced.*[4]

Draft value statements developed by individuals or committees that are then sent out for reaction don't meet these criteria. They may produce assent, but not ownership.

Shared values that provide common ground also need to be embodied. That is, they need to be put into action. Again,

Kouzes and Posner are helpful: "For values to be shared, they must be more than advertising slogans. They must be deeply supported and broadly endorsed beliefs about what's important to the people who hold them."[5] It is relatively easy to come up with a list of nice-sounding values. Everyone knows how we're supposed to act and treat each other. The real issue, however, is whether those nice-sounding words are taken seriously, whether they are embodied in the life of the organization and its people.

Values are important. That's clear. But what values are most important? Kouzes and Posner acknowledge three types of values that appear in "highly successful, strong-culture organizations."[6]

> High performance values stress the commitment to excellence, caring values communicate how people are to be treated, and uniqueness values tell people inside and outside how the organization is different from all others. These three common threads are central to weaving a values tapestry that leads to a shared commitment to greatness.[7]

Although Kouzes and Posner observed these values in secular organizations, they are clearly important in congregations, which also want to express the fullness of the kingdom, treat people as Christ did, and differentiate themselves from the general culture.

Language

It is impossible to underestimate the power of language. The continuing debates over gender-neutral and gender-inclusive language are testimony to that, as is the movement in the business world to change employees into "associates," bosses into "team leaders," and customers into "guests." Language can make a difference. It can change attitudes and shape behaviors. Certainly a name change all by itself means very little, but words do make a difference in the way we understand and respond to the realities we face. In DePree's words, they are one of the ways leaders define reality.

Kouzes and Posner remind us, "Leaders understand and are attentive to language. They know the power of words. The words we choose to use are metaphors for concepts that define what we hope to create and how we expect people to behave."[8] And again, "Leaders make full use of the power of language to communicate a shared identity and give life to visions. Successful leaders use metaphors and other figures of speech; they give examples, they tell stories, and relate anecdotes; they draw word pictures and they offer quotations and recite slogans."[9] The words we use can alienate or bring people together. They can narrow support or broaden it. They can create a reason for division or for common effort.

Robert Greenleaf expressed the importance of language this way: "Part of a religious leader's role as consensus finder is inventiveness with language and avoidance of a stereotyped style. One leads partly by the constant search for the language and the concepts that will enlarge the number who find common ground. A leader thus strives to bring people together, and hold them together, as an effective force. An experimental approach to language is a part of this skill."[10] This belief developed for him after he observed a course on "The Language and Literature of Leadership" taught in a university business school. The four history plays of William Shakespeare were used as case studies on the use of language by kings, language that helped them lead. While none of us has the advantage of Shakespeare as a speechwriter, all of us can grow, Greenleaf said, in our "sensitivity to language as an art form for effective leaders."[11]

In their book *How the Way We Talk Can Change the Way We Work*, Robert Kegan and Lisa Laskow Lahey of the Harvard Graduate School of Education also speak of the importance of language, especially as it helps create the common ground for leading change. "The forms of speaking we have available to us regulate the forms of thinking, feeling, and meaning making to which we have access, which in turn constrain how we see the world and act in it."[12] The language leaders use can develop forms of thinking, feeling, and meaning making that are narrow and exclusive or broad and inclusive. The broader and more inclusive our language is, the less constrained our view of the possibilities of organizational life and the stronger our common ground will be. They propose "seven languages of transformation," four that focus on personal change and three that focus on social change. They suggest that in moving from a commonly used language to a new and less restrictive one, leaders can strengthen and expand the common ground in an organization.

1. *From the language of complaint to the language of commitment.* Hidden beneath every complaint is something we care about. If we didn't care, we wouldn't complain. They explain: "This first transforming language enables us to make a shift from experiencing ourselves primarily as disappointed, complaining, wishing, critical people to experiencing ourselves as committed people who hold particular convictions about what is most valuable, most precious, and most deserving of being promoted and defended."[13] As the leader helps people in an organization shift from being "critical" to "committed," the focus shifts from complaint to possibility, and the common ground needed for change is created.

2. *From the language of blame to the language of personal responsibility.* Blaming encourages a desire to fix the problem as quickly as possible by getting rid of or changing the one who is at fault. Or, on the other hand, it encourages a hopeless fatalism that sees the organization as a victim of forces over which it has no control. As leaders help an organization overcome blaming as the way to deal with problems, they encourage a greater sense of personal responsibility to face the issues that confront the organization. This personal responsibility is the beginning point for developing a sense of shared responsibility for meeting the challenges the organization faces. This sense of shared responsibility—that we are all in this together and can do something about it—is another source of common ground.

3. *From the language of New Year's resolutions to the language of competing commitments.* Why are New Year's resolutions so hard to keep? They are about change, usually positive change—about commitments we want to make. And yet, by February 1, they are usually long forgotten. The problem, according to Kegan and Lahey, is fear—the fear of what may happen when we do what we say we want to do. This fear isn't something we need to (or even can) just get over. In fact, it most often betrays other commitments we have. If we are not aware of the existence of these other commitments, these other things we cherish, their power to offset our commitment to change continues to grow. In organizations, especially organizations seeking to change, it is important to talk about conflicting commitments—not only the new possibilities that change brings, but also losses, pain, and fear. As we do that, we broaden the ways people can connect to what is happening in an organization's life, and thus, we expand and strengthen the common ground.

4. *From the language of big assumptions that hold us to the language of assumptions we hold.* Big Assumptions, according to Kegan and Lahey, are assumptions that we assume to be true. They are never questioned. We believe they describe reality. If we do thing number one, then result number two will follow—no ifs, ands, or buts. Many of these Big Assumptions go back to our childhood and to the lessons we learned from our parents and in kindergarten about what life is like. But, Kegan and Lahey point out: "One thing is for certain: we will never have opportunity to explore whether the Big Assumption is true or not until we put it before ourselves where we can look at it, and begin to create a relationship to it."[14] As we create a relationship with it, we are able to analyze it and evaluate it. It begins to lose its power over us. This process is essential in organizations seeking to change, because quite often the Big Assumptions that some hold are powerful forces that lead to resistance to change. It is essential, but it is not easy: "It takes an extraordinary leader to cultivate a language for surfacing organizational

contradictions in a fashion that ends up not scapegoating some segment of the whole."[15] When it is successful, however, common ground is created as old Big Assumptions give way to new possibilities.

5. *From the language of prizes and praising to the language of ongoing regard.* There is a problem with praising, Kegan and Lahey tell us: "If we characterize people, even if we do so quite positively, we actually engage—however unintentionally—in the rather presumptuous activity of entitling ourselves to say who and how the other is. We entitle ourselves to confer upon people the sources of their worthiness."[16] The key to overcoming the problem is, according to the authors, being "non-attributive"—making statements that "do not characterize the other's attributes but rather describe the speakers' experience."[17] For example, rather than say, "You did a good job," say, "I appreciate the extra time you took to practice the music with me." Such "I-statements" work for communicating positive experiences as well as negative ones. They create a climate of regard within the community. This, too, becomes a way of strengthening common ground, because it affirms the importance of all those who contribute to the life of the organization and undercuts the presumption that some are entitled to be the arbiters of what is good or bad for the organization.

6. *From the language of rules and policies to the language of public agreement.*

Rules and policies are about compliance. People in the organization may comply, because their own sense of integrity leads them to follow the rules or because punitive measures will be taken if they do not. Either way, however, rules and policies are about an external standard. According to Kegan and Lahey, however, "the ongoing health of an organization actually depends upon leaders' abilities to foster processes that enhance the possibility of collectively experienced, public, *organizational* integrity."[18] The actions of those within an organization will be based on a common agreement that has been publicly affirmed and accepted, not upon rules that coerce conformity—in other words, on "shared values," or "common ground."

7. *From the language of constructive criticism to the language of deconstructive criticism.* Constructive criticism is all about one person—the person who is critiquing—claiming to have the right answer. Constructive criticism assumes that the person receiving it doesn't have a clue. Most often the one who gives is in a position of power. Even in the best of circumstances, the one who gives constructive criticism claims both power and responsibility. Every good personnel officer will tell you that when you offer constructive criticism to an employee, your responsibility is also to: "(1) say exactly what the person is doing wrong, (2) give the sense the criticism is meant to help, (3) suggest a solution, and (4) give a timely message."[19] The language of the leader can "deconstruct" this assumption of authority and responsibility as the leader moves away from offering criticism, creating a setting in which deeper learning can take place for all involved. A leader can do this simply by beginning a conversation with "I don't understand . . . ," rather than offering a critique of the other person's behavior. Again, this shift in language enhances common ground because it undercuts hierarchical relationships in which higher-ups are presumed to know more, and it affirms the insights and contributions that all in the organization have to offer.

The person who uses each of these "languages" seeks to develop a context in which change is possible. In doing so, these leaders can create and sustain common ground by providing a setting in which authority, responsibility, and power are broadly held and the experiences of a wide range of people are honored.

Story
Stories are a special form of language. In helping to establish common ground, they serve many of the same purposes as the effective use of language. Kouzes and Posner return to the importance of story time and time again as they discuss ways people develop their skill at the five exemplary practices their

research determined were essential for effective leaders.

> Stories serve as a kind of mental map that helps people know, first, what is important (purpose and values) and, second, how things are done in a particular group or organization. . . . Stories excite the imagination of the listener and create consecutive states of tension (puzzlement-recoil) and tension release (insight and resolution). Listeners are not passive receivers of information but are triggered into a state of active thinking as they puzzle over the meaning of the story and attempt to make sense of it, typically in reference to their own experiences and situations.[20]

Stories also play an important role in building a sense of commitment that is essential to common ground:

> Stories put a human face on success. They tell us that someone just like us can make it happen. They create organizational role models that everyone can relate to. They put the behavior in a real context. They make standards more than statistics; they make standards come alive. By telling a story in detail, leaders illustrate what everyone needs to do to live by the organizational standards."[21]

People from a great variety of backgrounds can see themselves in the story. When they do, the story provides a basis for common ground for those who might, at least on the surface, appear to have little in common.

In addition, stories have the ability to reach people at many levels of their consciousness. Research has shown that facts, figures, and policy statements have far less impact on decision making than stories, which always contain an emotional or affective dimension. A good story can motivate in ways that no chart or graph can. A good story allows people to feel themselves involved. It touches them, provokes them, encourages them, and perhaps even convicts them in a way that leads to deeper commitment to the common cause. As Kouzes and Posner put it: "Stories are better able to accomplish the objectives of teaching, mobilizing, and motivating than bullet points on an overhead."[22]

Stories are so essential to effective leadership that Kouzes and Posner offer a number of suggestions for what makes good storytellers:

- They tell personal stories about things and events they know.
- They tell stories about real people that have a strong sense of time and place.
- They tell stories in the first person, allowing their emotions to surface.
- They repeat the theme of the story.
- They keep the story short.[23]

Max DePree sums up his commitment to storytelling in these words:

Every family, every college, every corporation, every institution needs tribal storytellers. The penalty for failing to listen is to lose one's history, one's historical context, one's binding values.[24]

Every company has tribal stories. Though there may be only a few tribal storytellers, it's everyone's job to see that things as unimportant as manuals . . . don't replace them.[25]

Stories that share history and values with others are a major vehicle for building common ground in any institution.

Clearly story is essential to our faith experiences, for our faith is based in stories of Jesus, stories of God at work in the world. We'll explore those stories more fully as we move on to a discussion of what these secular insights mean for us as leaders in congregations.

Insights for Practice

Scott Cormode, associate professor of leadership development at Fuller Theological Seminary, provides a helpful Christian perspective on creating and sustaining common ground in his book *Making Spiritual Sense: Christian Leaders as Spiritual Interpreters*. Although its focus is meaning making, not common ground, many of the book's insights apply here. In the congregation shared meaning is built on a shared faith perspective. This does not mean adherence to a long list of specific theological beliefs or a doctrinal statement. Rather it is about a common perspective on life and its meaning that is drawn from faith resources. Certainly the Bible and overarching theological understandings are important in this view, but detailed agreement on specific points of doctrine is not. For example, belief in the divinity of Jesus would be an important basis of shared meaning in a Christian church, while literal belief in a virgin birth might well not be.

While acknowledging Max DePree's insight about the leader's role in creating reality, Cormode phrases it somewhat differently: "The first duty of a Christian leader is to provide a Christian perspective, an interpretive framework for people who want to live faithful lives."[26] This leadership task is one of helping people change their "mental models," the ways they look at the world. In Cormode's view, "The pastor's long-term goal is to help people to discover and internalize a specific interpretative framework, one that will make it possible to see all of life from a distinctly Christian perspective."[27] The interpretive framework people use to develop their own mental models, not necessarily the models themselves, provides the common ground in a congregation. That interpretive framework is based in a faith perspective that allows for broad and varied interpretation and yet still provides a common ground.

To understand why the interpretive framework can be the basis for common ground in a congregation, it's important to understand how we make meaning. A person takes the first step in the process, Cormode explains, "by focusing her or his attention on some things within a situation and by ignoring other things. The process begins, literally, with what a person sees—and what they fail to see. A person then arranges the things they see into a constellation."[28] Our expectations determine our selective seeing. More often than not, we see what we expect to see and ignore those things that challenge our expectations. The next step is to draw conclusions based upon what we have seen. Most often these conclusions are shaped by cultural understandings of reality, which often work unconsciously to form the meaning we assign to events. The meaning we assign then determines our actions.

This process of seeing, assigning meaning, and taking action based upon that meaning explains why it can be so difficult to identify common ground in congregations. Our expectations differ, depending on our life experiences and beliefs, so we see different things. The cultural stories we use to interpret what we see differ, so we assign different meanings. And because our meanings differ, we decide that different, often opposing actions are legitimate. It is most assuredly a formula for conflict!

And yet, attention to this process also helps us see how we can build common ground. Before discussing what leaders can do, however, it is important to acknowledge what we can't do. We cannot make spiritual meaning for others. Common ground cannot reside in a meaning leaders impose on others. Cormode elaborates:

> Instead leaders provide a theological framework that enables others to make their own spiritual meaning. Each person has to construct meaning for himself or herself. The pastor can only provide legitimated cultural tools—theological categories and spiritual vocabulary—that people can use as they each make their own meaning.[29]

In Cormode's view the greatest resource pastors have in performing this task is the preaching office. While pastors may bemoan their lack of authority in comparison to leaders in secular organizations, "in no other organization is there a custom that says for twenty minutes each week the assembled organization must sit quietly while the leader of the organization talks about whatever the leader thinks is important."[30] The sermon provides a significant way for leaders to share vision and values, and to use language and tell stories that become the "cultural tools" members of the congregation use in meaning making. In using these cultural resources leaders "seek to provide a theological framework that allows people to make new sense of their situation."[31] It certainly isn't possible to do that in one sermon, but with consistency and over time such a theological framework can be offered, and those who are listening may begin to use it to shape meaning in their lives. While it may begin with preaching, it doesn't stop there, for the preaching office "sets up ministers as theological interpreters in other congregational contexts as well."[32] And while it may begin with the pastor, it doesn't stop there either: "All Christian leaders—lay and clergy alike—bear a responsibility to provide theological interpretation for God's people."[33]

So, then, how does the leader provide a framework for members of the congregation to make meaning? We'll try to get a handle on that by returning to the insights we discussed earlier and using them to offer some perspective. All of this fits within the context of Cormode's understanding of the primary responsibility of meaning-making leaders: "give people the vocabulary and theological categories to imagine a different way to interpret the world and to construct a new course of action that flows from that interpretation."[34]

Vision

Vision is about purpose, the results a group hopes to achieve. It is, in Cormode's thought, one of the resources leaders can draw on as they seek to provide an interpretive framework for meaning making. In preaching, in teaching, in conversation, and in the newsletter, leaders can offer an underlying sense of purpose for the congregation's existence. As we've already seen, for vision to be truly meaningful it cannot be handed down from on high; it must bubble up from below. A vision discerned in that way does build common ground, because the process of discernment itself builds a broad-based understanding of God's call to the congregation. The role of vision in building common ground doesn't stop there, however. There is an important and continuing role for leaders to play in articulating that vision frequently and in exploring its possible implications. In doing so, the leader uses the vision of the congregation to reinforce a theological framework that makes both personal and corporate meaning making possible.

Values

Leaders also have an important role to play in articulating values espoused by the congregation. Again, as with vision, by doing this they help create a theological framework for meaning making that builds and strengthens common ground.

Certainly values are evident in Christian teaching and practice. The values that infuse the teachings of Jesus are ones the church holds up as norms for our living. There are also values by which each congregation conducts itself. Often similarities in these values can be lifted up and celebrated as a way to build common ground. In so doing, leaders are in effect reminding people of the things they hold in common and relating them to the tradition of the faith. Sometimes, however, biblical values and lived values are not the same. This disparity creates a tension that can also be effectively used by leaders to help build common ground. Recognizing the disparity and working to resolve it through the affirmation of commonly held values contributes another dimension to the theological framework that is used in meaning making. Dealing with a conflict of values is difficult work, a topic we'll explore further in chapter 9. If, however, this work is done with sensitivity, it provides an opportunity for thoughtful reflection on what is basic to the life of the congregation.

A helpful template for looking at values and deciding which ones to lift up and reflect upon can be found in the

three types of values noted by Kouzes and Posner which we
discussed earlier in this chapter: *high performance values,
caring values,* and *uniqueness values.* These are all present in
the values of the kingdom espoused by Jesus, and each has its
place in the church. High performance values, such as those
Jesus teaches about in the Sermon on the Mount, call us to
live as kingdom people and challenge us to live according to
the radical values of Jesus that focus on peacemaking, concern for the outcast, and service to others. Caring values are
most clearly present in the healing ministry of Jesus; they lead
us to practice genuine hospitality with others. Uniqueness
values present the church as a countercultural movement
challenging the customary ways of understanding the purpose for our living and success in life. Uniqueness values are
present in Jesus's teaching and living, but they are also apparent in the Book of Acts as the early church seeks to share
the gospel in an alien and often hostile world. This template
provides a way of looking at the values that are important in
a congregation and to assess those that are most significant
for its life. It can be an effective tool in the leader's effort to
build the theological framework that contributes to common
ground.

Language

The best language of faith is the language of metaphor. In
our words we are attempting to explain and contain something that cannot be explained and contained. So we resort
to images. By their very nature, images are open to a wide
variety of interpretations that can lead to confusion. Those
who want everything nailed down, those who want a place
for everything and everything in its place, will resist ending
the conversation with images. They will want the image dissected and interpreted, so that they can know what it "really
means." A leader seeking to build common ground will not
give in to the temptation to satisfy that desire.

The language of common ground should be open to nu-
merous interpretations, so that a wide range of people can

make their own meaning from it. Such language invites people to do that—not insisting, not provoking through guilt, not judging, but inviting. Invitational language is essential. Meaning cannot be forced upon anyone. Neither can anyone be forced to claim a common ground with others.

The language shifts suggested by Kegan and Lahey provide insight for our own use of language. Each of them leads to a more invitational, less dominating style of speech. If they are infused with appropriate theological content, they offer a way of providing the type of framework that Cormode maintains is essential for meaning making. The invitational aspect of the language is what encourages others to make their own meaning within the framework. But the presence of the framework provides the common ground that is essential.

As leaders shift their language along the lines suggested by Kegan and Lahey, they help set a context in which both authority and responsibility are more broadly felt. Remember, each of the shifts undercuts the traditional hierarchical understanding of power, communicates an honoring of the experiences of a wide range of people, and invites people to think more deeply about the ways in which they approach meaning making in their lives. Here are some possible ways in which these language shifts can encourage the building of common ground within a congregation:

- The shift from the language of complaint to the language of commitment invites people to see possibilities where they could see none before and encourages them to come together to make those possibilities realities. Leaders will talk more about the things people care about, even those evidenced in the things they complain about.

- The shift from the language of blame to the language of personal responsibility invites people to claim responsibility for their lives and the life of the congregation, recognizing that they are not victims. The shift opens people to experience the power of God at work in their midst, something that is impossible when the response to every challenge is blame. Leaders will talk more about what the congregation can do, pointing to possibilities that exist and can be seized.

- The shift from the language of New Year's resolutions to the language of competing commitments broadens the understanding of how all of us deal with competing commitments in our own lives. In doing that, it also encourages people to understand that competing commitments are not a threat to the life of a congregation but can in fact be the basis for growth. Competing commitments need not undercut common ground, so long as they are recognized as helpful to the congregation and its mission. Leaders will talk more about the varied commitments of members of the congregation in a way that honors them and recognizes the contributions they make to the congregation and its potential for ministry.

- The shift from the Big Assumption to assumptions I hold invites people to explore the nature of the Big Assumptions that shape their thinking and perhaps the corporate thinking of the congregation. Often these are barriers to the development of common ground within a congregation, because they work to narrow the space in which it is permissible to act. Leaders will ask questions about why people respond to situations as they do and make observations that encourage people to think more deeply about the reasons.

- The shift from the language of prizes and praising to the language of ongoing regard invites people to consider not their own skills and abilities, but rather what they contribute to the life of the community. It moves people away from an individualistic orientation toward a communal one and in so doing provides a basis for common ground. Leaders will talk more about the life of the community, the ways in which what people do and who people are enhance the possibilities for more faithful living and ministry.

- The shift from the language of rules and policies to the language of public agreement encourages a congregation to develop a common understanding of its life together and the values that will shape that life. It increases the sense of ownership of those values, even as it reduces a "rulebook mentality" in which common behavior is enforced by others. Leaders will talk less about the way people "should" act and more about the commonly held values that enhance the life of the community.

- The shift from the language of constructive criticism to the language of deconstructive criticism encourages a new understanding of power and authority in a congregation as it works to undercut assumptions that some people know more than others and therefore are in a position to determine the truths by which the congregation will live. Leaders encourage others to consider the meaning behind events and the motivation for their actions.

Taken together, these shifts in language encourage a greater sense of personal and corporate responsibility, a stronger sense of shared commitment, and a broader understanding of the congregation's diversity. In so doing, they contribute to the development of the congregation's life together, even as they also allow for greater freedom and more diversity. In Cormode's thinking, they are cultural tools that provide the framework people use to make meaning in their lives. The personal meanings may differ, but the framework provides common ground.

Story
Story takes the common-ground-building power of language one step further. The use of story provides the opportunity for diverse people to connect to a narrative in which they find meaning.

That shouldn't surprise Christians. The gospel story brings us together. We are at our best when we let the story unite us. We suffer when we begin to insist on specific interpretations of the story. Faith depends on story. It is as we enter the gospel story of the life, death, and resurrection of Christ and in it find meaning for our living that faith grows within us. This "story" is even more than what can be read from the Bible and told from the pulpit, however. It is also acted out in the rituals of the church. Communion, for example, is the acting out of the gospel story of God's love and sacrifice that enables new life. Because both story and ritual permit a variety of interpretations, Cormode maintains, "this allows people to find meaning in the same story or ritual even if they interpret the story or ritual in quite divergent ways."[35] Story and ritual become a source of common ground.

The leadership task in working with stories is to enable people to see themselves in the story. This happens as a congregation is helped to interpret the story. Cormode argues, "Stories need an interpreter, someone to update them with contemporary examples that bring the story to life. . . . And when a preacher helps people imagine themselves into a story, then they are motivated to live out that story in their daily lives."[36] As leaders help others link their own life experiences to the biblical story, they aid them in growing in their faith. And yet at the same time, because the same story is open to different interpretations by different people, the story itself provides a point of common ground.

Every congregation has its own stories. The leader's task is to listen carefully to those stories and to find ways to tell them that make connections to the broader gospel story. In this way people can begin to see the way the life and ministry of their congregation connect to the story of God's work in the world. As a congregation struggles to determine the values that will shape its life together, the story of the years in the wilderness following the Exodus can help members see the way God is at work among them even in the midst of that struggle. Or if members of a congregation have a sense that the changes in the world of the past few years have left them disoriented and without a clear understanding of the ways faith can be real, the story of the Exile and a people who sang "How shall we sing the Lord's song in a foreign land?" can help them understand their experience in new ways.

One of the stories of the congregation I serve, one that was all but lost in more recent stories of struggle, concerns the founding of the church in 1809. The community of Plymouth in those days had rigorously retained its Pilgrim heritage, and there were only Congregational churches in town. First Baptist was the first church not of the "established order." As such, the clergy of the town saw it as a great threat to religious and moral life. One of them, Adoniram Judson, Sr., is reported to have said, "What are we to do with these Baptists? They are turning the town upside down." As the years went on, his son went off to India as a Congregational missionary but on the voyage became convinced that the Baptist understanding of baptism was the correct one. He became the first Baptist missionary. His father followed his lead, became a Baptist, and shortly thereafter became the pastor of our congregation. One of my efforts as pastor as we approach the two-hundredth anniversary of our founding is to tell this story and to connect our experience as a congregation to all those biblical stories of the ways people of faith have continually turned towns upside down. In doing this, we can build a common ground for a new sense of identity and purpose, one that connects not only to our own history but also to the great story of faith of which we are a part. Members of the congregation may have different ideas about what it means to turn the town upside down and how that might be done today. That is the meaning they bring to the story. But the story itself establishes a common ground for our life and ministry.

Leadership Styles

In this chapter we have explored some of the factors that contribute to creating and sustaining common ground.

Remember, though, that the common ground we need is one that provides stability in a time of change. Often, however, as a congregation seeks to continue to be faithful in today's world, it may confront the need for a change in the very things that we have said help build common ground—vision, values, language, and story. This doesn't necessarily mean that the old needs to be abandoned, but rather that something new needs to be added, or that the old needs to be reinterpreted in some significant way.

One insight we can draw from this chapter is that a number of sources of common ground are present in a congregation, and that although one may need to undergo change, we can continue to draw on the others to sustain common ground. Continuity in one area provides the stability that is needed as change takes place in another. The leader's task is to lift up the sources of common ground even as she or he encourages change. The discussion of leadership styles found in *Primal Leadership* offers several important insights for performing this rather difficult balancing act, and it is to that we now turn. We'll use the perspective offered by the discussion of leadership styles to suggest that creating and sustaining common ground for change may necessitate the use of several styles at the same time. Let's look at an example.

If establishing a new vision is a primary need in a congregation, but the members lack the ability to enter into a vision discernment process, pacesetting leadership in this area may be needed. If the past has locked the congregation into stultifying patterns of behavior, undercutting its ability even to think about new possibilities, a pacesetting style of leadership can help it move out of this rut by demonstrating new ways of carrying out ministry. At the same time, however, as the need for a change in vision is becoming apparent, a focus on values, language, and story will help maintain common ground. For this, something other than a pacesetting style is called for. The use of a coaching style may help individuals identify with the values of the congregation. The use of a democratic style related to story may encourage the broader telling of the stories that frame the identity of the congregation. In each of these areas the style must be determined by the ability of congregation members to assume the responsibility of dealing with the concern. Because maintaining common ground depends upon broad involvement, it is particularly important to ensure that some of the styles used encourage participation, even if that is not possible in all areas of the congregation's life.

Building common ground is a highly complex activity. It is virtually impossible for any leader to take all factors into account and devise the perfect leadership strategy. The insights offered in this chapter can, however, enable us to assess the current situation and develop an approach to leadership that will enhance the common ground within a congregation even as we work to encourage change.

CHAPTER 7

Empowering Others

Power! Power! Who's got the power? The question reverberates in every congregation. Sometimes the words are unspoken (because nice Christians aren't concerned about power), but still the reverberations are felt. They influence every dimension and dynamic of congregational life. There are power blocs within the laity. Power is sought by clergy (sometimes masquerading under the seemingly more appropriate name "pastoral authority").

Loren Mead, former president of the Alban Institute, has written about the importance of clergy foregoing the power they exercised within the congregation under the Christendom paradigm.[1] Congregational consultant Bill Easum has written about the need for control that motivates some laity.[2] Countless others have contributed to the discussion. It's unlikely that we'll be able to resolve many of the issues related to power in one brief chapter. We will, however, try to make some sense of them in the hope that a better understanding of what's at stake will put us, as congregational leaders, in a better position to exercise power appropriately.

Before we look at what secular writers have to say on the subject of empowering, let's understand a key assumption about power upon which our discussion will be based: The power that we as leaders hold in a congregation is God's power, to be used for God's purposes. Jesus himself confronted the temptation to misuse power. Even he had to get the power issues worked out before he could begin his ministry. Parker Palmer, in his reflection on Jesus's wilderness temptation in Luke 4:1–15, warns against the illusion that power does not corrupt—that it is somehow a neutral force that can be used for good or ill depending upon the moral fiber of the user.

> Power . . . has a life of its own. Once we have seized it, it seizes us, and wrestling ourselves from its grip requires superhuman effort. If power over things seems at first like a tool, those who hold it may soon become tools wrapped in power's own strong hand.[3]

Palmer calls attention to the essential reality about power from a Christian perspective: "Power and glory are not the devil's [or anyone else's] to give. They belong to God alone, and only through God can we share in them."[4] Whatever power we hold must be power, in Palmer's words, "with and for others."[5] Recognizing the inherent corrupting nature of all power, our aim as leaders is always to share power as broadly as possible—to give it away as much as possible and sometimes simply to refuse to use it. We do not empower others. Only God empowers. For us, empowering others involves creating the setting in which they can draw upon God's power to accomplish God's purposes.

With that idea as background, let's take a look at what some secular writers have had to say about power and empowering.

Insights from the Theories

Secular theorists provide a helpful perspective on forces that enable and block empowerment in an organization.

Enablers of Empowerment

In chapter 2 we discussed Ronald Heifetz's distinction between technical and adaptive work. In the adaptive challenges that congregations face today, a primary leadership strategy must be giving the work back to the people. It is only as members encounter and address the realities of their situation that they can begin to develop appropriate responses. To do this, they must be empowered to think and to act. This means, of course, that they must also be disabused of any notion they may have that an "expert" will rescue them from their plight by providing the answers. That is why empowerment is a central leadership practice in today's church. Because the insights needed for adaptive change (or, from a faith perspective, to discern God's new thing at work in our midst) can come only from the people themselves, the members of the congregation must be empowered to seek these insights, declare them, and begin to live out of them.

Kouzes and Posner see the empowering of others as essential to effective leadership in today's world, but they also recognize that the power is not really the leader's in the first place:

> It is not a matter of giving people power—it's liberating people to use the power and skills they already have. It's a matter of setting them free, of expanding their opportunities to use themselves in service of a common and meaningful purpose. What is often called empowerment is really just letting people loose, liberating them to use their power.[6]

Leaders do this in a variety of ways, they explain.

> Exemplary leaders make other people feel strong. They enable others to take ownership of and responsibility for their group's success by enhancing their competence and their confidence in their abilities, by listening to their ideas and acting upon them, by involving them in important decisions, and by acknowledging and giving credit for their contributions.[7]

The authors point to four leadership essentials in empowering others:

1. Ensure self-leadership by giving power away so that others can act.

2. Provide choice so that others make the decisions that will determine how their work will be done.

3. Develop competence and confidence by providing training, sharing information, and coaching people as they fulfill their responsibilities.

4. Foster accountability, so that people will clearly understand their interdependence.[8]

Robert Quinn, whose insights we have explored at several points, describes two views of empowerment that he sees operating in institutions; the mechanistic and the organic. The assumptions of the mechanistic view:

- Start at the top.
- Develop a clear vision, plans, and assignments.
- Move decisions to the appropriate levels.
- Provide necessary information and resources.
- Encourage process improvements.

Quinn summarizes these assumptions: "In short, empowerment is about *clarity, delegation, control, and accountability.*"

The assumptions of the organic view:

- Start with the needs of the people.
- Explore the difficult issues.
- Model integrity through risk taking.
- Encourage initiative.
- Build teamwork.

He summarizes: "In short, empowerment is about *risk, growth, trust, and teamwork.*"[9]

Empowerment can, in fact, happen both ways. If we look at these two views from the perspective provided by Heifetz's understanding of technical and adaptive work, the mechanistic view lends itself most clearly to technical work in which the answer is clear and the task of the "expert" who provides that answer is to mobilize others to implement it. The organic view, however, relates more to adaptive work in which there is no clear answer and people need to be empowered to discover it.

Citing a study of four hundred managers at Fortune 500 companies, Quinn describes four dimensions of empowerment. To be empowered people need a sense of

1. meaning (what they are doing is important to them)
2. competence (they are confident about their ability)
3. self-determination (they can choose how they will do the work)
4. impact (what they do makes a difference)[10]

This study also defined four organizational conditions that lead to an empowering environment:

1. clear vision and challenge
2. openness and teamwork
3. discipline and control
4. support and a sense of security[11]

Noting that conditions 1, 2, and 4 are a part of the organic view of empowerment, while condition 3 is an expression of the mechanistic view, Quinn maintains that both views are essential to meaningful empowerment.

Quinn concludes his discussion by sharing a "final key," which has a decidedly familiar ring to it: "We do not, however, empower people. Empowerment cannot be delegated. We can only develop an appropriate empowering environment where people will have to take the initiative to empower themselves."[12]

If we cannot empower people, how are they empowered? In *Primal Leadership* Daniel Goleman and colleagues share a "self-directed learning theory" that provides some helpful insights. Self-directed learning (the kind of learning needed for empowerment) begins with personal assessment, reflecting a key question:

- Who do I want to be? (my ideal self)

It then moves through a series of steps that lead to personal change and empowerment:

- Reflecting on the present reality
- Who am I? (my real self)
- Where do my ideal and real overlap? (my strengths)
- Where do my ideal and real self differ? (my gaps)
- How do I build on my strengths while reducing my gaps? (my learning agenda)
- Experimenting with new behavior, thought, and feelings
- Practicing the new behavior, building mastery
- While this is taking place, continually developing trusting relationships that help, support, and encourage each step in the process[13]

In the next section we will offer a faith perspective on these steps. For now, however, we can acknowledge that they provide a critical insight into one significant way people can be empowered.

Barriers to Empowerment

Before moving on to the implications for leadership in the

church, we need to consider the other side of the coin—the factors that inhibit empowerment.

John Kotter identifies four primary barriers to empowerment:

- formal structures that make it difficult to act (think: the need for redundant board/committee/council approval before anything is done)

- a lack of skills that impedes action (think: little financial support for training for ministry both within and outside the church, with the possible exception of the pastor's continuing education budget)

- personnel and information systems that make it difficult to act (think: the control of information by informal systems based on friendships and alliances)

- bosses who discourage actions aimed at implementing new ideas (think: pastors and other leaders who don't want anything, especially anything new, done which they cannot essentially control)[14]

Robert Quinn also notes a significant barrier to empowerment. He calls it "the tyranny of competence." Those who do things well keep doing them, because they believe they can do them better than anyone else. Often they can. They also believe it is just plain easier to do it themselves. Often it is. Competence becomes a tyranny when it undermines empowerment. It demoralizes others, shuts them out of any opportunity to learn, and reinforces the belief that no one else is needed. Often organizations are blind to the tyranny of competence, believing that all is well because things are getting done in good fashion, but unable to see the cost. It might be well for congregational leaders (especially pastors) to consider the ways in which their very competence undermines the empowerment of others (especially laity).

With that note of caution, let's consider the implications of these theories for the life and ministry of the congregation.

Insights for Practice

As we move our discussion of empowerment to the congregation, it's important to have a common understanding of what we are empowering people to do. Too often we think of empowerment in the congregation as empowering laity to assume new roles (often roles traditionally played by clergy) in the institution. We think about empowering volunteers to do more work more effectively. We think about empowering people to assume a greater role in the congregation's decision making. This is an accurate, yet severely limited understanding of empowerment in a Christian context. Our aim is really to empower people to assume their role in God's mission in the world, to experience the full and abundant life that is Jesus's promise by becoming the people God created them to be. For some, empowerment may indeed have something to do with their involvement in the church. But it's a whole lot bigger than that.

Let's return now to the steps of the self-directed learning shared by Goleman and colleagues. If we do not empower others but they empower themselves, then self-directed learning is one way to think about the process. As people of faith, however, if we believe that people do not empower themselves but are empowered by God through the work of the Holy Spirit, then we need to understand this process from a faith perspective. To help us do that I want to draw on some thoughts from my book *Traveling Together: A Guide for Disciple-Forming Congregations*,[15] which presents the concept of discipleship as a lifelong, ongoing process of growing in relationship with God and living out more fully God's intentions for our lives as we participate in God's mission in the world. It suggests an understanding of discipleship that contains three elements: deepening, equipping, and ministering. Deepening involves growing in relationship with God, self, and others. Equipping is about discerning gifts and call, and developing skills and knowledge. Ministering is action—participating in God's mission in the world. Growth as a disciple happens (or, one might say, we are empowered to be disciples) as we are engaged in all three areas. All are essential.

With this understanding of discipleship as background, it is possible to note some significant relationships between self-directed learning and empowerment for discipleship.

SELF-DIRECTED LEARNING	DISCIPLESHIP
My ideal self—Who do I want to be?	Deepening—Who is the person God created me to be?
My real self—Who am I?	Deepening—What is the reality of who I am?
My strengths—Where do my ideal and real selves overlap?	Equipping—What gifts, skills, and knowledge do I have that help me live out the person God created me to be?
My gaps—Where do my ideal and real selves differ?	Deepening—Where do I miss the mark in being the person God created me to be? Equipping—What unrealized gifts do I have?
My learning agenda—How do I build on my strengths while reducing gaps?	Equipping—What gifts, skills, and knowledge do I need to develop?
Experimenting with new behavior, thoughts, and feelings	Equipping—What is God calling me to do? Ministering—How do I live out that call?
Practicing the new behavior, building mastery	Equipping—How do I grow in my use of my gifts, skills, and knowledge? Ministering—How do I use my gifts, skills, and knowledge in God's mission?
Developing trusting relationships that help, support, and encourage each step in the process	Deepening—How do I grow in relationship with others in community?

With this faith perspective on the process of empowerment, we can move on to take a look at the presence of blocking and enabling forces within the congregation—forces that enable empowerment or block empowerment. The framework for this discussion comes from a workbook, "Empowering Laity for Their Full Ministry" by Dick Broholm and John Hoffman (Laity Project at Andover Newton Theological School, 1981).[16] Although some of its content is dated, its basic framework remains compelling and helpful.

The nine blocking/enabling forces the workbook identifies are:

- consciousness raising
- gifts and call
- support and accountability
- spiritual formation
- language and liturgy
- validation
- roles and structures
- education
- content of ministry

Let's explore the ways each of these addresses the insights raised by secular writers and informs this leadership practice in the congregation.

Consciousness raising. We are empowered for what? That is the key question related to consciousness raising. Empowerment can never reach its potential as a leadership practice without a clear understanding of the purpose for which people are empowered. The core of the understanding is that empowerment is more about mission in the world than work in the church. All Christians are called to ministry. For some, that ministry is in the church. For most it is not. The basic theological concepts of the priesthood of believers and the ministry of the laity need to be understood in their fullness before empowerment can happen. That is what consciousness raising means in this context.

Commissioning services provide the opportunity for consciousness raising for people in regard to using their gifts in ministry and seeing the need for the congregation as a whole to provide support for that ministry. The task is not easy. Some members resist being commissioned, even for such ministries as hospice care and work that addresses the needs of children in our society. Often those who might be commissioned see their participation in such a service as boasting about themselves rather than seeing the service as the congregation's celebration of the power of God at work in their lives.

Gifts and call. The discussion of discipleship based on my book *Traveling Together* lifted up the central importance of gifts and call to empowerment. Discovering gifts is a vital part of the self-directed learning process. According to the authors of the Laity Project report, "If the gifts and calls of laity are not affirmed, the church and its members are weakened."[17] When Kouzes and Posner speak about empowerment as "liberating people to use the power and skills they already have," they are talking about discovering gifts. When Quinn talks about the need for a "clear vision and challenge," he is talking about a sense of call.

Gift inventories offer one approach to discovering gifts, but their use can be dangerous. Most of them demonstrate a narrow understanding of gifts and translate those gifts into specific jobs that can be done within the church. Few broaden their perspective enough to encompass a full understanding of the ministry of the laity. In addition, the very nature of a survey is mechanistic. Better is a more organic approach in which people look for the gifts of others and begin to name them. What about replacing the nominating committee with a "gifts-discernment team"? Equip team members with an understanding of gifts and turn them loose in a congregation.

When Kouzes and Posner talk about empowerment as "letting people loose," they mean finding ways to help them discover and use what is there already—the gifts that God has given them.

Support and accountability. According to Kouzes and Posner, one of the four leadership essentials in empowering others is to foster accountability, so that people will clearly understand their interdependence. Accountability is often interpreted as "people checking up on you." That's not what I'm talking about here. I'm suggesting the cultivation of a group of people who care about you and what you are doing, and with whom you can honestly discuss what's happening in your life, faith, and ministry. Quinn speaks about the importance of openness and teamwork, discipline and control, and support and a sense of security in creating a climate that lends itself to empowerment. These are all aspects of empowerment. Broholm and Hoffman explain:

> There is a critical link between empowerment for ministry and accountability for ministry. When Christian laity become clear about their ministries and communicate with each other about their call, they tend to feel accountable to the believing community for the way they steward their gifts and energies. This sense of accountability adds support and encouragement to one's ministry.[18]

Teams are essential to empowering people for ministry because they provide this kind of accountability. It is all but impossible to go it alone, although that has most often been our practice for ministries within the congregation. Rather than assigning individuals to visit people, however, we know that a better way is developing a team whose members visit but who also meet together to share and pray and learn. That same principle can be applied to those who are called to ministry in the world. Perhaps a group of people in similar occupations can be formed, or a group of people who share only a desire to talk about being a Christian in the workplace. The team provides the support and accountability that are essential to empowerment.

Spiritual formation. Our spiritual lives provide a primary source of power for ministry. This is the growing-in-relationship-with-God dimension of deepening. Although this dimension is missing from secular writing, some authors express a growing sense that being in touch with the spirit within is an important element in empowerment. In chapter 3 I talked about Robert Greenleaf's concept of *entheos*, the power that motivates. Other secular authors write about the importance of meditation in developing the resources needed for effective work. Christians have a unique perspective on spiritual growth, to be sure, but the concern is shared by many others.

Again, however, it is important to recognize the importance of teams in spiritual formation. Often we think about spiritual formation as something we do on our own. In the words of the Laity Project report, "Although it is a deeply personal activity, spiritual formation must also be a collective process."[19] So, part of empowerment in a congregation is the development of groups that focus on the use of spiritual disciplines and spiritual growth.

Language and liturgy. I discussed the importance of language in chapter 6, relating it to creating and maintaining common ground. The insights there also apply to the importance of language in empowering. The new dimension here is liturgy, especially the worship experience of the church. If worship is about empowering people for mission in the world, then it must have a worldly dimension. Worship needs to use resources from the secular world in both its content and style. It needs to be indigenous to the lives of the worshipers. Otherwise, people will be less likely to connect their experience of worship to the realities they face in everyday life. The use of illustrations in sermons can contribute to this indigenous worship, as can the use of music, films, and other contemporary cultural expressions.

Worship is important to empowerment also because it involves the whole people of God in one of the most important dimensions of their life together. Broad involvement is therefore needed in both shaping and leading worship. The Laity Project report observes, "Worship is not the work of the people of God if all the shaping and expressing are done by one individual or group."[20]

Validation. The Laity Project report maintains, "Because we believe God seeks to call all to Christian ministry, we need a means to confirm laity's response."[21] By confirming the ministry of the laity, congregations respond to Quinn's understanding of the importance of people's sense that what they are doing is important and makes a difference. Ordination provides this validation for clergy. Commissioning has the potential to do the same for laity. But we have too often restricted commissioning to people who are getting paid by the church for the ministry they perform. Without some form of validation, it is difficult for many people to see their work as real ministry. It is difficult to understand our work in the world as "full-time Christian service."

Roles and structures. Three of John Kotter's four barriers to empowerment relate to roles and structure: formal structures that make it difficult to act, personnel and information systems that make it difficult to act, and bosses who discourage actions aimed at implementing new ideas. What's true in the secular world is also true in the church, as noted in the Laity Project report: "For the most part, church roles and structures do not affirm, support or empower laity whose primary ministry is in the secular world."[22] "The existing roles and structures imply that ministry is what occurs around the church building."[23] Most church structures are concerned with institutional maintenance. Sometimes participation in these structures is called ministry, but it still has a significant maintenance dimension—maintaining the Sunday school, maintaining the youth group, maintaining all the programs that keep the institution alive and well. Certainly lives are changed by these programs, and people grow in them, but most programs still focus attention on the church and its ministry, not on disciples and their ministries. The switch from maintenance to ministry is the change needed.

This change is not just about structure, however. It's also about role and the way leaders conduct themselves in their various roles. Quinn's concept of the tyranny of competence is important here. If in our role as leaders we continue to provide answers, even if they are good ones, we are undercutting others' participation in the life of the congregation, their own ability to grow in ministry. When we stop giving answers and ask people what they think, the question may well lead to frustration. It may even lead some to think that we are not doing our job or that we must be incompetent. The result, however, may well be a new understanding of the roles of clergy and laity in the congregation.

The congregation I serve has a long tradition of pastors with varied theological orientations and experiences. One of the parishioners' great strengths is openness to this diversity. As I became more familiar with the congregation, however, I began to realize that another dimension of this openness was a lack of clear identity. The members were willing to follow the lead of the pastor because they were not clear about who they were and what they wanted to do. I had a decision to make. I could provide clear leadership in a direction I believed in, with every expectation, based on their past experience, that the members would follow. Certainly I was competent to do this, and the members were willing. On the other hand, I could work to encourage them to decide what they wanted to do. That would mean refusing to be clear about the specific direction I believed the church should take, not giving answers about what to do. I've opted for this second approach. All of us have struggled with it to some extent. My conviction is that I am providing the space for the congregation to gain a new understanding of itself and of God's call. This approach depends, however, on my willingness to refuse to play a significant part of the customary role of pastor.

Education. The only one of Kotter's four barriers to empowerment that doesn't fit in the discussion above fits here: the lack of needed skills undermines action. Kouzes and Posner address this concern as they talk about the importance of developing competence and confidence by providing training, sharing information, and coaching people as they fulfill their responsibilities.

As with most issues of ministry, the way we handle this one, the importance we place upon it, is reflected in the church budget. If we take training for ministry in the world seriously, how is that reflected in the way we spend our money? Most church budgets have money for clergy and staff continuing education. Many have money to train those who fill positions in the church, such as Sunday school teachers. Sadly, I don't know of a single church (although I trust there are some) that provides funds to support people in training for the ministry to which they are called in the world.

There's more to equipping people for ministry than developing skills, however. The Laity Project puts it this way: "A special need exists for methods of theological reflection which enable the resources of faith to be brought to bear on contemporary circumstances in ways which inform practical decision making and help us to mature as Christians."[24] We need to begin to help people to think theologically, to reflect on their lives from the perspective of faith to understand what God is asking of them and how God is supporting them.

Content of ministry. This final blocking/enabling force is about the theology of ministry. This is how Broholm and Hoffman put it:

> Most Christian laity are unable to claim what they do for their life's work as "ministry." Even if we accept the theological premise that *all* Christians are called to "full-time" ministry, we often cannot relate the concept to our own lives. A major reason for this inability is we have limited knowledge and understanding of the nature and content of ministry beyond the institution. Because the church focuses primarily on religious vocations such as pastor, missionary, and church administrator or educator, we are uninformed about the particular forms of unordained ministry.[25]

The reality that congregations are "uninformed about the particular forms of unordained ministry" brings us to the issue of the ministry we have been given by Christ: what are we here to do? While there may be broad agreement that we are engaged in ministry, the precise nature of that ministry is unclear. Where does it happen? Who does it? The challenge as we seek to empower people for ministry is to broaden our usual understandings of what it is and to help members build connections between their everyday lives and Christ's call to ministry in the world.

Building these connections is one of the most significant sources of confidence in laity as they engage in ministry in the world. If they can see what they do as part of God's mission of the redemption of all creation, they will grow in the awareness that they are linked to a grand and ultimately important purpose. The deep sense of confidence that comes from being engaged in the work of God in creation is essential to the empowerment of all of us for ministry. Kouzes and Posner talk about the importance of self-confidence for empowerment in the workplace. What they say, however, is equally true for all who seek to become empowered for ministry in the world.

> Without self-confidence, people lack the conviction for taking on tough challenges. The lack of self-confidence manifests itself in feelings of helplessness, powerlessness, and crippling self-doubt. Building self-confidence is building people's inner strength to plunge ahead in uncharted terrain, to make tough choices, to face opposition and the like because they believe in their skills and in their decision-making abilities.[26]

And for people of faith, we can add: because they believe in the power of God at work in them to fulfill God's mission in the world.

CHAPTER 8

Working with Groups

Small groups shape the life and ministry of every congregation. Much attention has been given recently to the development of a "small-group ministry" and its importance in deepening the life of faith. These groups are important, no doubt, but other types of groups also exist in congregations. In this chapter we'll be looking particularly at study/support/sharing groups, ministry teams, and boards and committees.

Most of the secular literature talks about work teams in the office setting. While this literature provides some valuable insight for us, in this chapter we'll look in depth at resources that focus specifically on groups in the congregation. As we look first at the secular literature, we'll focus on what it has to say about factors that are important for all types of groups: trust, purpose, task and maintenance needs, and leadership. When we look in more detail at congregational resources, we'll explore these four factors and add spiritual life to the mix.

Insights from the Theories

The dynamics of the workplace and the congregation are decidedly different. We've encountered this reality in each chapter, but it is nowhere as apparent as in the discussion of groups. Workplaces are not focused on issues of faith and growth, two primary concerns of groups in the congregation. There are some similarities: For example, both workplace teams and ministry teams are concerned with doing or producing something. But even then, the internal dynamics of the group are markedly different. Groups in the church, for example, are made up primarily of volunteers and lack the typical workplace power dynamics that are involved in employer-employee and boss-worker relationships. This means we need to be careful when transferring secular insights about groups to the congregation. Rather than seek a comprehensive understanding of what secular writers have to say about groups, we'll simply pull a few key insights that will inform our discussion of groups in the congregational setting.

Trust

Trust is essential to community. As such, it is essential to every practice we have discussed. We'll talk about trust here, however, because in the secular literature, trust is most often discussed in relationship to groups.

What leads to trust in a group? Clearly the presence of trust is linked directly to the way in which participants relate to each other. One of the best descriptions of trust-building behavior I have heard came in a training event I attended years ago. The leader encouraged all participants in the group to be "open, honest and direct; willing to be seen and heard; caring about yourself and others." Her guidance sounds simple enough, but those of us who have tried it know it never comes easy. If participants act in a trustworthy way, trust will develop in a group. But for participants to do that, the group's leaders must first be trustworthy. Without leaders who are both trusted and trusting, groups members cannot trust.

Kouzes and Posner address trust in their discussion of developing a collaborative spirit in an organization:

> At the heart of collaboration is trust. It's *the* central issue in human relationships within and outside organizations. Without trust you cannot lead. Without trust you cannot get extraordinary things done. Individuals who are unable to trust others fail to become leaders, precisely because they can't bear to be dependent on the words and work of others. So they either end up doing all the work themselves or they supervise work so closely that they become overcontrolling. Their obvious lack of trust in others results in others' lack of trust in them.[1]

The authors point to several key factors in the leader's role in developing trust in a group. First, as noted, the leader must be willing to trust others—to demonstrate the nature of trust, to take the risk of trusting first so that others can and will follow. Second, they stress the importance of leaders' being open to influence, considering alternative viewpoints, and letting others exercise influence over group decisions. They observe, "By demonstrating an openness to influence, leaders contribute to building the trust that enables their constituents to be more open to their influence. Trust begets trust."[2] This openness leads, then, to the third significant factor: "becoming vulnerable by trusting in others whose subsequent decisions we can't control."[3] Finally, they underscore the importance of listening as a way to demonstrate sensitivity to people's needs and interests.

Developing trust takes time. Susan Wheelan, professor of psychological studies at Temple University and author of *Creating Effective Teams*, sees trust as a key component in the development of a working group. She presents a four-stage theory of group development. In Stage 1 (Dependency and Inclusion) the focus is on personal issues related to participation in the group, and the group relies almost exclusively on the leader to provide direction as these issues are worked on and resolved. It is important that the leader in this stage is both trustworthy and trusting. In Stage 2 (Counterdependency and Fight), group members begin the trust-building process, most often through conflict about group norms and purpose. Wheelan observes: "In a Stage 2 group, trust is just beginning to build. Members have not developed enough faith in the trustworthiness of their colleagues to be certain that a sub-set of them would work for the good of the whole group."[4] Wheelan explains Stage 3, "Trust and Structure," this way:

> If a group manages to work through the inevitable conflicts of Stage 2, member trust, commitment to the group, and willingness to cooperate increase. . . . This third state of group development is characterized by more mature negotiations about roles, organization, and procedures. It is also a time in which members work to solidify positive working relationships with each other.[5]

Stage 4 (Sustaining High Performance) requires ongoing attention to trust, ensuring that it is nurtured, especially when events threaten to undermine it. In all four stages of group life, growing and sustaining trust is a determining factor in a group's ability to function effectively.

Stephen Covey offers an insight that helps us understand yet another dimension of trust: competence.

> Trustworthiness is more than integrity; it also connotes competence. In other words, you may be an honest doctor, but before I trust you I want to know that you're competent as well. We sometimes focus too much on integrity and not enough on personal competence and professional performance. Honest people who are incompetent in the area of professed expertise are not trustworthy.[6]

Trusting the competence of the leader comes first, but the concern eventually extends to trust in the competence of all group members to assume the responsibilities involved in the group's purpose.

Purpose

Every group exists for a purpose beyond being a group. It may be to produce a product, to solve a problem, to create something new, to discover new possibilities, or to grow in new ways. Clarity about that purpose is essential to the effective functioning of the group. It reduces the chances of the group's unraveling in conflict or losing its focus. The purpose of the group needs to be something that matters. Clarity about something no one cares about won't suffice. The group needs to be clear about a purpose that is deemed worthy by its members.

Robert Quinn defines a team as "an enthusiastic set of competent people who have clearly defined roles, associated in a common activity, working cohesively in trusting relationships, and exercising personal discipline and making individual sacrifices for the good of the team."[7] For a group to be an effective team that displays these qualities, it must have a worthy purpose held in common. A group may do some things together. It may have trusting relationships among members. Working effectively in a sustained effort over time, however, takes more than that. The purpose of the group determines the nature of the competencies and roles needed. It motivates the personal discipline and individual sacrifices required for a group to function effectively as a team for a sustained period of time.

Kouzes and Posner underscore the need for a commonly held purpose that is deemed worthy by group members if they are to develop a sense of being "all in this together."[8] Without this sense, a team cannot function effectively. In the authors' view, the key to developing such a purpose is ensuring that it is based on shared goals shaped by the group's vision. When the vision and goals have established a common ground, it is possible to develop a shared purpose considered worthy by group members.

Task and Maintenance Needs

Every group must attend to two basic needs: its work (the task need) and its life together (the maintenance need). Fran Rees, a management consultant, describes those needs this way:

> Teamwork has two dimensions: task and social. These two dimensions are inseparable, for without either, teamwork does not exist. The task dimension refers to the work that team members are to perform—the jobs they have to do and how they are going to do those jobs. The social dimension refers to how team members feel toward one another and their members on the team.[9]

In her book *How to Lead Teams,* Rees shares ten essentials of teamwork that focus on both task and maintenance needs. The list, while including a number of items related to the achievement of the group's task (such as goals and power to make decisions), also emphasizes items related to group life. These include maintenance of individual self-esteem, interaction and involvement of all members, and mutual trust. To make the importance of both task and maintenance abundantly clear, Rees specifically includes attention to both process and content as one of the ten essentials.[10]

While focusing on task issues that enhance the productivity of teams, Susan Wheelan also stresses the importance of maintenance issues. One of her ten keys to productivity is communication and feedback.

> High performance teams have an *open communication structure* that allows all members to participate . . . get *regular feedback about their effectiveness and productivity* . . . [and] give each other *constructive feedback about individual performance and contributions* . . .

Finally, *a high performance team utilizes feedback about team processes and productivity to make improvements in how it is functioning.*[11]

The balance of task and maintenance is essential in groups. Many congregations tend to err on one side or the other. They become so focused on the job to be done that they forget the needs of the people. Or, on the other hand, they become so concerned about the people and their feelings that their ability to accomplish God's work suffers. And in many congregations both can be cloaked in enough virtuous-sounding piety that it may be difficult to establish and maintain the balance that is needed.

Leadership

Groups cannot function without leaders. Each of the three areas of group life we have discussed depends upon a leader who guides the group in building trust, clarifying a worthy purpose, and attending to both task and maintenance concerns. But the leader cannot do it on his or her own. Even within the more traditional hierarchical setting of the office, a single leader cannot do it alone if teams are to function effectively. Fran Rees puts it this way: "The new leader-facilitator focuses on creating a workplace that encourages everyone to take responsibility for the success of the company."[12] To achieve this shared responsibility, the leader listens, asks questions, directs group process, coaches, teaches, builds consensus, shares goal setting, shares decision making, and empowers others to get things done.[13] The leader's role is much more one of facilitating than of directing. And yet, as our discussion of trust demonstrated, the effective leader is a clear and important presence in a group, influencing its direction, guiding its purpose, and attending to its life.

Recognizing that groups are interactive systems, Susan Wheelan reminds us, "Leaders alone cannot be held responsible for group success or failure."[14] Goleman and colleagues see this interactive system as "the power of the tribe: the tight

cohesion that people feel when there are long-standing collective habits and a shared sense of what they hold sacred."[15]
Leaders have a vital role to play but also need to recognize
the limits of their influence and responsibility. If they fail to
do so, the chances are great that they will fall into a counter-
productive style of more authoritarian leadership as they seek
to achieve their goals for the group. The authors comment,
"One of the biggest mistakes leaders can make: ignoring the
realities of team ground rules and the collective emotions of
the tribe and assuming that the force of their leadership alone
is enough to drive people's behavior."[16]

With these insights from secular writers as background,
let's now consider our leadership role as it relates to study/
sharing/support groups, ministry teams, and boards and
committees in the congregation.

Insights for Practice

Something is happening to the role of groups in the church.
Formerly clear distinctions between study groups, prayer
groups, mission groups, task forces, and committees are blur-
ring. Study, prayer, ministry, and maintenance are happening
everywhere and in all sorts of ways. This emerging reality
is the background against which our discussion of leading
groups takes place. Of course, some boards of trustees still
believe they are about the "business" of the church, so Bible
study (or even prayer) need not be a part of their meetings.
And certain task-oriented people believe that a group is
wasting time if it allows for personal sharing in its meetings.
Nonetheless, change is taking place.

A number of factors have contributed to this changing landscape. In *Congregational Megatrends*, Jeff Woods,
pastor and denominational executive, notes the shift from
secondary planning to primary planning in congregations:
"Successful church events are no longer planned by bringing
together representatives of various congregational groups

who have little or no interest in the topic on the table."[17]
What this means is that planning by elected boards charged
with responsibility for specific, segmented areas in the life of
the congregation, areas in which they may not have a personal commitment, is becoming increasingly less effective. In
contrast, "primary planning involves putting together a team
that has a vested or primal interest in the topic."[18] A decreas-
ing sense of obligation to the institution, increased diversity,
and generational differences all contribute to this new reality. In today's world, primary planning based in teams that
come together around a specific concern and exist only until
that concern has been addressed are more effective vehicles
for ministry within a congregation than elected, long-term
boards and committees.

In addition to this shift to primary planning, even groups
charged with specific ministries are shifting away from being exclusively task-oriented. The members of a short-term
team planning an event about which they are passionate will
support each other in their shared passion. Longer-term ministry groups, such as a worship team, are increasingly becoming the primary place of belonging, support, and study for
members. The opposite shift is taking place as well. Groups
that at one time might have been seen exclusively as study
or support groups are discovering ways to serve others as
they share their experience and invite others to join them.
The groups that participate in the "shawl ministry" in many
congregations provide an illustration of this blending of purposes. The shawls knitted by group members and given to
those in need offer a significant ministry. The sharing that
takes place when the group gathers to knit creates a web of
mutual support. The prayers and blessings offered by group
members for the shawls and the people to whom they are
given bring a spiritual emphasis to the group. Similarly, in
my own church, as we establish a care team to visit and support church members and friends, we are shifting responsibility from the elected board of deacons to a group that is
gifted and called for this specific ministry. As they begin to

meet, our hope is that members will not only engage in the task they have assumed, but will also share with each other, pray together both for each other and those they visit, and develop more skills for the ministry they have taken on.

Tom Bandy offers a helpful way to picture this multifaceted dynamic of groups.[19] He suggests that all groups within a congregation need to include prayer, action, learning, and sharing—PALS. Groups will emphasize different facets at different times, but all should be present to some extent in every group all the time. Increasingly, groups in the congregation are moving toward this more comprehensive understanding of their functioning. As they do so, the expectations for leaders change, and the number of people able to lead groups effectively needs to increase. Knowing how to run a meeting and being familiar with Robert's Rules of Order are no longer sufficient. It's not enough simply to be a good Bible teacher or an adept organizer of people to work on a project. As the nature of groups becomes more comprehensive, so do the essential skills of leadership.

As we consider the leadership role in small groups, we need to discuss two distinct areas: first, the qualities and skills needed by those who lead groups; and second, the qualities and skills needed by those who will encourage the development of more comprehensive small groups in a congregation.

Leading in Groups

Small groups in a congregation should be settings where we speak the truth in love to build up the body of Christ for the work of Christian service (Eph. 4). Small groups provide one of the primary sources of community in a congregation. There are, to be sure, other ways to belong, but many people find that their sense of being part of a congregation rests in the relationships they have in a small group.[20] Small-group members can also provide significant pastoral care for one another. Jeff Arnold, pastor and church consultant, notes an even broader possibility for pastoral care: "A small group which provides ministry to its members contributes to the overall care that churches should offer their members. But small groups can also help shoulder the burden of care within the larger body as well."[21] Many small groups not only care for themselves, but reach out to others in need in the congregation and the community.

For both caring and reaching out, the qualities of small groups identified by the secular writers we looked at are all essential. Groups require trust, a sense of purpose, attention to both task and maintenance, and leaders skilled in guiding a group. But leaders in the congregation need to bring something else to the leadership of small groups—a spiritual dimension, the perspective of faith.

Corinne Ware, in her book *Connecting to God: Nurturing Spirituality through Small Groups*, offers an essential insight:

> We do not bring God to us by means of something we achieve. . . . We can only experience the God who is *already* there. Our efforts, then, are to enhance openness and availability. Spirituality is deepened by access. It is not God who is unavailable. It is you and I.[22]

The spiritual focus of groups, then, is always an effort to attune group members more fully to the presence of God in their midst.

One simple way to begin this attunement is with Tom Bandy's insight regarding prayer, action, learning, and sharing. We'll use this framework to guide our thinking about working with groups in the congregation. It suggests first that one of the leadership tasks is to step back and look at the ways the group attends to each of these four activities. If groups are, in fact, doing all four, it's likely that the important spiritual dimension of group life is in good shape. Part of the group leader's task, then, is to encourage the group to practice all four dimensions in ways appropriate to the group's purpose. That means stressing activities that relate directly to the group's purpose, but also not ignoring those that might otherwise be forgotten. The worship team needs to study as well as plan its ministry. The shawl-ministry group needs to pray as well as knit. The care team needs to increase its visitation skills as well as pray for those in need. The Bible study group needs to act on what it has learned in some specific way.

Remember, when we talk about small groups, we include in our discussion study/sharing/support groups, ministry teams, and boards and committees. Whether formal or informal, mandated by the constitution and bylaws, or part of a programmatic effort, all these groupings can be based in prayer, action, learning, and sharing. These qualities are most readily apparent with study/support/sharing groups. For many of these groups prayer, learning, and sharing are already a regular part of their life. The stretch for them will be to consider how they might be involved in action, what ministry they might have. These groups tend to be inwardly focused. Action will encourage them to look outward to see how their group experience can be shared with others. They might start another group. Or they could adopt a project that relates to concerns they have been sharing with each other. Remember, this new involvement in action needn't (and most likely shouldn't) become the primary focus of the group. But as they move into action, the group members become engaged in ministry to others, acknowledging this dimension of their Christian life and thereby deepening their spirituality.

This same blend of prayer, action, learning, and sharing should be present in ministry teams. The four facets can shape the life and ministry of a team, whether its focus is planning worship, leading the youth group, building homes, visiting, or doing any other ministry. Because of the ministry focus of these teams, action is already a part of what they do. Here the movement might be to ensure that prayer undergirds their ministry by making it a regular and natural part of their life together. Taking time to share important life events and experiences also serves to enhance the effectiveness of a team that is working together in ministry. And as the team works together, it will also need to learn together—whether that be about the biblical basis of its ministry or the skills that team members need to engage in their ministry more effectively.

Established boards and committees will face the greatest challenge in moving in this direction. The patterns of work and ways of conducting business are well established in these groups. Often, too, they see themselves doing business and not ministry. In his helpful book *Transforming Church Boards into Communities of Spiritual Leaders,* Charles Olsen, consultant and founder of Worshipful Work: Center for Transforming Religious Leadership, suggests a number of ways to encourage a greater spiritual focus in board and committee work. One approach is to make prayer a vital part of all meetings. This can be done in a number of ways:

- *Pray about items on the agenda.* "Entrust the stuff of a meeting to God in the same way you prepare for sleep—by letting go."

- *Intersperse prayers of thanksgiving.* "Follow each committee report or grouping of stories with prayers of thanksgiving."

- *Glean for prayer.* "At the beginning of a meeting you might assign . . . people to keep notes with an eye toward separating out items for prayer."

- *Offer prayers of confession.* "Confession covers not only errors and sins, but also weariness, frustration, confusion, elation, boredom, fulfillment, and so forth."

- *Sing prayers.* "Send each board member home with a church hymn book and the assignment to select one verse of any hymn that best captures the most appropriate prayer for the church at this present time."

- *Take "time out" for prayer.* "Time out periods could be called by a strict clock setting by the meeting moderator or by any member who requests it at any time for any reason."

- *Rotate prayer.* "At the beginning of the meeting assign each person to a certain fifteen-minute segment of the meeting; during that assigned time, members should pray silently for each person in the group and for the deliberative process in which the board is engaged."

- *Acknowledge subliminal prayer.* "Prayer may be ceaseless and subliminal, even when we engage in active work or deliberation."[23]

Understanding the work of boards and committees as "worshipful work," Olsen also suggests that agendas can be built using the format of an order of worship, or a candle can be lit as a sign of God's presence.

The primary work of boards and committees is to discern God's call to the congregation. Olsen envisions that discernment happening when boards and committees function in this way:

- Every member of this board is daily working at discerning God's will in her own life.

- The board has bonded as a community through the stories of life and faith board members have told and their common experience of the grace of God.

- The meetings are conducted in a framework of worship.

- Members have agreed on the priority matter at hand and are willing to take six month to study, reflect, and pray toward a decision.

- The moderator of the group is fair and sensitive.

- The decisions made are not necessarily the most convenient, cheap, politically palatable, or agreeable to the pastor's wishes.

- Decisions are agreed upon with one consideration: that God is leading and calling out this particular form of obedience and mission.

- In response to the leading, board members prayerfully work to implement the decision, all the while trusting that God will accomplish more than they ever imagined.

- The board maintains a playful spirit, not taking itself too seriously. It is open to celebrate at the drop of a hat what God is doing.[24]

It is a great vision! The amazing thing is that it can become a reality—if there is openness and if leaders are ready and able to lead in this direction.

Leading toward Groups

In addition to guiding groups in their spiritual growth and enabling them to work more effectively, leaders need to move a congregation toward viewing groups as a primary way of being. This task includes developing small study/sharing/support groups, as well as shifting to ministry teams to handle much of the work of the congregation.

One of the first requirements is training people to lead groups. The more groups a congregation has, the more group leaders it needs. Deliberate attention needs to be given to providing training and experience in leading groups. This process can begin in simple ways. The church I serve has a long history of study groups led by the pastor. Often the group was a Bible study—it was assumed that the pastor knew more about the Bible than the laity did. I began to adjust the focus of the Bible study away from sharing information to sharing ways in which the passage related to our lives. In this, all of us were the "experts." We then moved away from Bible study to book studies in which we would all read a chapter or two between meetings. My leadership at this point focused on basic process questions rather than content. It even became something of a joke that I began each meeting by asking, "So what do you want to talk about from this week's reading?" The next step was to ask others to lead the group. Many did not want to. Others, however, figured that if leading was just a matter of asking some questions, they could do it. Of course, skilled group leadership involves a lot more than that, but this approach did begin to help members realize that people other than the pastor could lead a group. From there we could begin to work on developing additional skills. We do that more in casual conversations in which we reflect on what happened in the group than through formal training experiences. This approach is not for every congregation, but it fits both the reality and style of our congregation. The point for everyone, however, is that movement toward the development of group leaders can happen in simple and natural ways. You don't necessarily need to develop a "small-group ministry" and provide formal training sessions for a crop of small-group leaders.[25] There is certainly nothing wrong with that approach, if it fits the congregation, but it need not happen that way.

Another strategy that can lead to the development of small groups in the church is to be as permission-giving as possible. If someone has an interest in studying a new book or in reaching out to the homeless, rather than going to a board for approval, encourage that individual to gather people who share the same interest and start a group. Significant ministry has happened in congregations simply because someone stood up in worship one day and said, "I'm interested in . . ." If anyone else is, please let me know."

Small groups can also be an effective strategy for board and committee work. Rather than having the entire board or committee plan and implement a project, encourage the board to appoint groups to do it. In using this approach, it is vital to provide a clear mandate for the group's work along with authority to do it. Remember the importance of primary planning that we talked about earlier. Continuing, detailed oversight by a board will destroy any group's passion for its work. In giving the group its mandate, encourage group members to make prayer, action, learning, and sharing part of their life together. If one board member is a member of the group, that person might attend to this responsibility. If the board itself has previously been attentive to these dimensions of its own life, the translation to the group will be relatively easy. As more people experience this approach to group life, it will come more naturally to every group that is formed.

We cannot avoid addressing one issue raised by the increasing use of small groups in the church—one that affects our own leadership. The more small groups a congregation has, the less control leaders have. That means we need to look honestly at ourselves and our own need to be in control. If that need is severe, we will be reluctant simply to turn people loose. We may cloak our reluctance in all sorts of positive explanations, such as "staying focused" and "avoiding chaos" and "using our limited resources wisely," but if our own need to be in control of what happens is at work, small groups have no chance of being successful. Our ability to encourage the development of small groups depends on our ability to trust others. Kouzes and Posner challenge us to that kind of trust with these words: "When leaders create a climate of trust, they take away the controls and allow people to be free to innovate and contribute. Trusting leaders nurture openness, involvement, personal satisfaction, and high levels of commitment to excellence."[26]

Once that kind of trust has been established, the key to developing spiritually grounded groups in the life of a congregation is having a clear understanding of their role and importance. There are any number of ways to encourage their development. Sometimes we may need to work around traditional structures and simply establish new groups. Sometimes we may need to bend the bylaws a bit. There is no doubt, however, that opportunities to encourage the development of small groups will continue to present themselves. The leader's role is to take advantage of those opportunities to enhance the spiritual life and mission effectiveness of the congregation.

CHAPTER 9

Dealing with Institutional Stress and Conflict

This chapter is not about conflict resolution. It is about the inevitability of conflict and the need at times to nurture conflict to help a congregation to be faithful to God's call in today's world.

Of course, conflict resolution is an essential skill for congregational leaders. Resources for resolving conflict abound.[1] These resources suggest processes for both avoiding and resolving conflict, which at times can be an exceedingly complex challenge. In one way or another, all of them boil down to the insight provided by Daniel Goleman and his colleagues:

> Leaders who manage conflicts best are able to draw out all parties, understand the differing perspectives, and then find a common ideal that everyone can endorse. They surface the conflict, acknowledge the feelings and views of all sides, and then redirect the energy toward a shared ideal.[2]

Rather than explore the various insights and processes that make conflict resolution possible, in this chapter we'll look at the ways in which leaders in a congregation can use

conflict. Despite the ideal image of the loving, peaceful congregation in which everyone is happy—an image deeply ingrained in most all of us—leaders at times need to encourage
conflict. They need to act in ways that make conflict inevita-
ble. They need to enhance, not reduce, conflict. Doing these
things is difficult. Few of us enjoy conflict. For many of us,
taking deliberate actions that will lead to conflict runs counter to both personal desire and our image of our role in the
congregation. The very thought of it may make our stomachs
tighten, our hearts pound, and our palms sweat. And yet, at
times inciting conflict is what effective and faithful leadership demands.

Insights from the Theories

In this section we will look at secular writers' insights on the
need for institutional stress and conflict and positive ways
for dealing with it. With that as background, we'll turn in the
next section to specific ways we can implement their insights
in our congregations.

The Need for Stress and Conflict

The beginning point for our discussion is Ronald Heifetz's
theory of adaptive change (see chapter 2). The leadership
role in facing an adaptive challenge is not to provide answers, because no one knows what answers are needed to
address the concerns the organization is confronting. The
key to discovering the answers is giving the work back to the
people, so that the answer can emerge from their experience.
What do the people have to offer that enables this answer
to emerge? In a word: conflict. The appropriate responses
to adaptive challenges most often emerge out of a conflict
of values within the organization. Sometimes the conflict is
between values held by different groups. Sometimes it is between professed and lived values. But the answers needed
nearly always emerge from a conflict of values. Without the

conflict, there can be no answer. Heifetz and his colleague Marty Linsky remind us: "Deep conflicts, at their root, consist of differences in fervently held beliefs, and differences in perspective are the engine of human progress."[3]

While Heifetz provides a helpful framework for understanding the importance of institutional stress and conflict, others also point to the positive role they play in organizational change and the important role of the leader in bringing them to the surface. In *Leading Change*, John Kotter reflects on sources of complacency in organizations, including low performance standards, a focus on narrow goals, a lack of sufficient feedback, a kill-the-messenger culture, the natural human capacity for denial, and too much "happy talk" from senior management.[4] In such a situation it is the role of leaders to challenge the culture of complacency by acting to develop a sense of urgency.

> Establishing a sense of urgency is crucial to gaining needed cooperation. With complacency high, transformation will go nowhere because few people are even interested in working on the change problem. With urgency low, it's difficult to put together a group with enough power and credibility to guide the effort or to convince key individuals to spend the time necessary.[5]

Leaders can create a sense of urgency by allowing a crisis to develop, setting high standards of achievement that cannot be met without significant change, encouraging conversation with unsatisfied customers, using outside consultants to encourage more honest conversation, and stopping the "happy talk."[6] These behaviors all challenge complacency, increase the sense of urgency, and in so doing create stress and conflict. Again, it is the leader's responsibility to create (or at least bring to the surface) institutional stress and conflict, so that needed change is possible.

Similarly, in *Leading in a Culture of Change*, Michael Fullan acknowledges the important role that resistance plays in leadership. "In a culture of change, emotions frequently run high. And when they do, they often represent differences of opinion. People express doubts or reservations and sometimes outright opposition to new directions."[7] This is the stuff of which institutional stress and conflict are made. Fullan brings a new dimension to the discussion with the insight that this "resistance" not only creates the conflict or sense of urgency needed to promote change, but also provides insight into possibilities for the future.

> Leaders in a culture of change welcome [this resistance]! They certainly re-frame it as having possible merit, and they almost always deal with it more effectively than anyone else. Defining effective leadership as appreciating resistance is another . . . remarkable discovery: dissent is seen as a potential source of new ideas and breakthroughs. The absence of conflict can be a sign of decay. . . . [There are] many examples which illustrate that allowing (even fostering) negative feedback is a step (not the only one) to needed improvement.[8]

When we listen carefully to the resistance, the conflict of values Heifetz talks about becomes clearer. With greater clarity about that conflict, it is possible to develop the new ideas and breakthroughs Fullan sees within resistance to change.

In many organizations conflicts, especially conflicts related to the organization's purpose, are avoided at all costs. Deeply ingrained attitudes and behaviors are transmitted, usually nonverbally, about the way one should behave so as not to provoke disagreement. Avoiding conflict, however, is one way to ensure the slow death of the organization, because if disagreements are not faced, there is no possibility of the kind of change that will enable the organization to renew itself. In this situation the leader's role needs to be one that encourages conflict. The leader doesn't create the conflict, of course. It is already there. What the leader does is bring it to the surface—usually by refusing to engage in the conflict-avoidance behaviors that are the accepted norms of the organization. The leader may simply ask questions about the issues or reflect upon what seems to be underlying stress in the organization's life. Sometimes a more direct approach may be needed, such as deliberately raising issues that everyone else is avoiding, because everyone else fears that any discussion of them will provoke disagreement.

Ways to Deal with Stress and Conflict

None of the insights we've just discussed suggest that conflict is always a good thing. They shouldn't be taken as a rationale for deliberately antagonizing people about anything and everything. Focused conflict at a controlled level enables the answers needed for positive change to emerge. Unbridled conflict about secondary issues doesn't help at all.

Heifetz suggests that the first task in using conflict positively is the creation of a holding environment. "A holding environment is a space formed by a network of relationships within which people can tackle tough, sometimes divisive questions without flying apart. Creating a holding environment enables you to direct creative energy toward working through conflicts and containing passions that would easily boil over."[9] A holding environment is maintained through a set of structures and procedures that provide boundaries. Sometimes the common ground that has been established in an organization provides the needed holding environment. If there is clarity about shared vision and values, these can provide a sense of security because people know that whatever else changes, they can count on these to remain. Sometimes the holding environment is provided by an outside person who can set boundaries—someone who isn't personally engaged in the struggle. A consultant brought in to lead a strategic planning or discernment process, for example, can offer a sense of confidence because the community senses it is in the good hands of someone who knows what she is doing. Ritual can also help create space that can be a holding environment. Worship often provides this element in congregations. No matter what else is happening, people can rely on worship to be a life-giving, life-sustaining element of their life together. A holding environment may take many forms, but it always functions to contain and limit the stresses that are a part of adaptive change. Heifetz notes: "The point of a holding environment [is] not to eliminate stress but to regulate and contain stress so that it [does] not overwhelm. People cannot learn new ways when they are overwhelmed. But eliminating the stress altogether eliminates the impetus for adaptive work."[10]

Heifetz offers a number of guidelines to enhance the possibility that conflict within the holding environment will be productive.[11] Three of these are particularly important for us. First, *identify the adaptive challenge*. Leaders should be clear about the changes needed in an organization and focus the discussion on issues related to this adaptive challenge. What shift is needed in the way the organization identifies itself, the way it relates to its setting, the approach it takes to its work? The differing opinions about this challenge reveal different values. If the leader is not clear about what the adaptive challenge is and does not focus the organization's work on that challenge, it is exceedingly difficult to focus the conflict in a way that will be helpful.

Second, *keep the level of distress within a tolerable range for doing adaptive work*. Heifetz and Linsky refer to this guideline as "controlling the temperature." Some measure of stress and conflict is essential to change. Without it, there is no reason to change. And yet too much stress and conflict can overwhelm a system and those within it. If the level of stress is too great, people will simply shut down and abandon work on the challenge. You can raise the temperature when you "bring attention to the hard issues . . . keep it focused there . . . let people feel the weight of responsibility for tackling those issues."[12] You can reduce the temperature in a number of ways, such as dealing with technical problems that are more easily handled, creating successes to celebrate, coming at the problem from a different and less threatening perspective, or taking more of the responsibility on yourself.

These are all temporary measures, however, designed to turn down the temperature on stress and conflict for a while. After an appropriate rest, when coping resources have increased, it will be time to turn the temperature up again.

The third guideline Heifetz offers to increase the chances of productive conflict is to *focus attention on ripening issues and not on stress-reducing distractions.* This is a bit different from controlling the temperature. Here the concern is work-avoidance mechanisms that redirect attention away from the adaptive challenge and consume time and energy. Heifetz's list of these mechanisms includes "denial, scapegoating, externalizing the enemy, pretending the problem is technical, or attacking individuals rather than issues."[13] Because these redirect the issue away from the adaptive challenge, they undercut the possibility of productive conflict. In contrast to lowering the temperature, these mechanisms do not provide reduced stress to gather new resources but redirect the focus completely away from the challenge the organization faces. And in the process they often increase stress.

If the role of leaders is to instigate, encourage, and enhance institutional stress and conflict, they need to be prepared to suffer the consequences. The not-very-pleasant reality is that if leaders are instrumental in bringing conflict into the open and increasing stress in an organization, much of the uneasiness, resentment, and anger created will be directed toward them. But, as I've said before: It's not about you. Heifetz stresses the importance of distinguishing between self and role: "A person who leads must interpret people's responses to his actions as responses to the role he plays and the perspective he represents."[14] Comments and emotional responses directed toward the leader are not personal—they may sound that way, but in truth they are aimed at the leader's role. Heifetz and Linsky explain this concept in more detail: "The people in your setting will be reacting to you, not primarily as a person, but as the role you take in their lives. Even when their responses to you seem very personal, you need to read them primarily as reactions to how well you are meeting their expectations."[15]

If your actions seem to be creating conflict and increasing stress, it's safe to assume that most people will conclude that you are not meeting their expectations. Negative reactions are likely. Being able to make this distinction between self and role doesn't automatically eliminate the leader's feelings about the way others respond, but "it enables an individual not to be misled by his emotions into taking statements and events personally that may have little to do with him."[16] Even personal attacks are not really about you. Reacting to them as personal can have the detrimental effect of moving the focus of the work to you and away from the adaptive change needed. "Reacting defensively to the literal substance of personal attacks colludes with the attackers by perpetuating the diversion. This work avoidance mechanism almost always succeeds simply because it's so natural to take a personal attack personally."[17]

Making the distinction between self and role is not easy. Acting upon that distinction can be even more difficult. It takes both self-knowledge and a strong sense of self-worth. Heifetz and Linsky offer helpful insight into this reality: "By knowing and valuing yourself, distinct from the roles you play, you gain the freedom to take risks within those roles. Your self-worth is not so tightly tied to the reactions of other people as they contend with your positions on issues."[18]

Kouzes and Posner provide additional insight; they explore the concept of psychological hardiness, which enables leaders in high-stress situations to remain healthy. Although they are dealing with physical health, their insights apply also to the mental well-being needed to distinguish between self and role. In the study they cite, three factors were most important to leaders:

1. *A belief that they could influence the direction and outcome.* "Lapsing into powerlessness, feeling like a victim of circumstances, and passivity seemed like a waste of time to them."[19]

2. *A strong commitment to the process.* "They were curious about what was going on around them, and this

left them to find interactions with people and situations stimulating and meaningful. They were unlikely to engage in denial or feel disengaged, bored, and empty."[20]

3. *A challenge to grow.* They believed "personal improvement and fulfillment came through the continual process of learning from both negative and positive experiences. They felt that it was not only unrealistic, but also stultifying to simply expect, or even wish for, easy comfort and security."[21]

Leaders who had these qualities were able to deal effectively with the stress of their leadership positions and to remain healthy doing so. These same qualities help to ensure a mental well-being that enables leaders to maintain a healthy distinction between self and role even amid significant stress.

Insights for Practice

Let's acknowledge the difficulties up front. First, most of us who are leaders in the church do not like conflict. It goes against our nature as caring people. Second, the image we have of the congregation as a community of faith usually does not feature conflict in any significant way. Third, those involved in congregations are dealing with stress and conflict in many areas of their lives and neither want nor need more conflict when they come to church. If church is a place of stress and conflict, they might just stop coming.

I hope the previous section of this chapter has made clear the need for institutional stress and conflict if the church is to survive in these times of tumultuous change. That's a good beginning point. We can quit trying to come up with excuses for why stress and conflict aren't needed and focus our attention instead on how we prepare ourselves to undertake them and help the congregation deal with them.

Part of the reality of the pastor's life is his or her awareness of the issues that create stress in the lives of people in
the congregation. Such an awareness may be present to some
extent for all leaders in a congregation, but pastors are often
more deeply conscious of these issues than most. Knowing
that people you care about are already dealing with the financial stress of being laid off from work or the emotional stress of a troubled teenager or the stress of a difficult
marriage—or any number of other life situations that create
stress—makes it difficult for a pastor to decide to enhance
the stress level within the congregation. More than anything
else, it seems, these people you care about need church to be
a place in which they can find some measure of escape from
the problems they face, some measure of peace. Even if you
believe everything we discussed in the previous section, it is
difficult to act intentionally to increase their stress.

This difficult reality is one of the ongoing struggles of my
own ministry. It often seems that to be compassionate means
to forego dealing with the issues essential to the vitality of
the congregation. The longer I have lived with this tension,
however, the more I've come to see that this way of looking
at the situation hides a deeper reality. Time and again I've
discovered a close parallel between the issues causing stress
in an individual's life and the issues that need to be addressed
in the congregation. The people are the congregation, after
all, and the dynamics that shape their personal lives often
shape congregational life as well. The connection between
family systems and congregational systems described by
family-systems therapist Edwin Friedman in *Generation to
Generation* provides an important insight for us here. While
the surface issues may differ in many cases, the underlying
and most significant issues in both personal and congregational life are similar. Working on the issues in one area has a
positive impact in the other. Thus raising the level of institutional stress needs to be seen as something more than adding
to the stress of already stressed-out people. It may well be
that, of course, but it can also provide a setting in which it is

possible to address concerns in a way that will have a significant and positive impact in people's personal lives.

The congregation, for example, may struggle over balancing the budget or venturing into a new ministry to which many believe God is calling them. To bring this issue into the open and to encourage dealing with it will increase stress. But it will also help the congregation deal with important issues related to the balancing of material concerns and God's will. In doing this it can have a direct impact on the way people in the congregation deal with similar tensions in their own lives.

The relationship is not always clear, but I am coming to believe that an important connection exists between the issues that create stress in our personal lives and those that create stress in the congregation. If the congregation can handle these issues appropriately in its life, this effort will have a significant impact on the lives of members. Yes, it still increases stress, it still means that the congregation won't be a place of refuge and peace, but it does hold out a real possibility of important growth. For me, this belief doesn't eliminate the tension I feel about this issue, but it does provide a significantly different perspective from which to consider it—one that offers added reason to endure the stress.

Heifetz's concept of the holding environment is an important one for us as we consider institutional stress and conflict in the congregation. Before we even begin to raise the difficult issues, we need to have done our work in establishing this holding environment. The key, says Heifetz, is trust: "Trust in authority relationships is a matter of *predictability* along two dimensions: values and skills."[22] Again, let's at least note in passing that there are "who" and "what" dimensions to trust—the "who" of values and the "what" of skills. The essential question is this: Do members of the congregation have reason to trust me? Have I demonstrated both values and skills that lead them to have confidence in me as both a person and a leader? There is no quick way to accomplish this task. It takes time—more in some settings than in others.

If a congregation is conflicted, if it has been mistreated or abused by previous leaders, developing trust will take a significant amount of time. But the time must be taken, because without the trust that is key to a holding environment, it is not possible to deal with the stress of adaptive change.

Beyond the development of personal trust, two other areas are important to consider when developing a holding environment in the congregation: pastoral care and worship. Pastoral care—being with and for people in Christ's name—enhances relationships. As it does that, it builds a trust that ensures people that you care for them, are concerned about them, and love them even if you disagree with them, even if you are the reason for stress in their lives. The trick here, of course, is not to allow pastoral care to be so consuming that it makes leading adaptive change impossible. At times in congregations the demands for pastoral care become the "stress-reducing distractions" I mentioned earlier that are used by some to ensure that significant issues will not be dealt with. It takes a wise leader to sort out the distinction and act accordingly.

Worship can also contribute to the development of a holding environment. The weekly reenactment of the rituals of the faith, the telling of the story, the preaching of the word, the sharing of bread and cup—all these provide a basis for trust, a time and place to affirm what matters most and continues to hold the community together. I've thought often in recent years about the "worship wars" that seem to engulf so many congregations. It seems ironic that one of the great resources of the church that can be used to provide a context for significant change has instead become a battleground. I can't help wondering if careful attention to and identification of the deeper adaptive change that the congregation faced would have shifted the focus away from worship and allowed the congregation to use worship to contribute to the development of a holding environment that makes significant change possible.

Finally, we need to note the importance of distinguishing between self and role. This task is essential, and yet it is extremely difficult to accomplish. The understanding of call that led clergy into ministry and that brings others to leadership in the congregation is intensely personal. It informs our identity, making it all but impossible to make a distinction between who we are as people and our role as leaders in the faith community. Clergy find it particularly difficult, I think. Is there a time when you are not a pastor? Can you stop playing that role when the workday is over? Is it so much a part of you and your identity that distinguishing between self and role is all but impossible? And yet, laying aside the pastoral role is essential.

I first began to get some insight into this tension in my own life and ministry when I served as an interim pastor. I couldn't help noticing that I approached this responsibility very differently from the way I approached serving as the full-time pastor of a congregation. I began to realize that as a pastor, too much of my identity (my ego) was tied up in what happened in the congregation. It wasn't difficult to see just about everything as a personal reflection on me and my ministry. Under those circumstances, it was difficult to distinguish between self and role. Everything about me was invested in what happened in the congregation. I did take things personally. I did find it difficult to gain perspective. I suffered because of it. My family suffered. And the congregation suffered.

For a part-time interim, such delusions were easy to avoid. There wasn't enough time to look after everything. Days in every week were concerned with something other than the congregation. I had a clear identity apart from being the pastor of the church. That didn't mean I wasn't pastoral with the members, but "pastor" was clearly a role I played. I don't mean "playing a role" in the sense of acting, artificially becoming something I wasn't. Rather it was a role in the sense of a responsibility I took on, using my experience, gifts, and skills to be an important presence in the midst of the congregation. I'm convinced that this is a much healthier way to relate to a congregation. I am certain my family appreciated the change immensely! And I know that I was able to accomplish some important work in the congregation as members prepared for a new pastor.

Not everyone struggles with this issue in the way I have, I'm sure. But my sense is that nearly all of us are aware at times that our ego investment in our role as pastor and leader is greater than it should be and that we have lost the ability to define ourselves apart from the role. This is perhaps the greatest issue in the "who" of leadership. It brings us full circle, back to the first practice—attending to self. If we cannot do that, all the other practices become merely skills to develop, work to be done. We may reach great heights that way, but we will always have to wonder if we have really been the people God created us to be, if we have served others the way God called us to serve.

Ministry in all its forms is a wondrous thing. For both clergy and laity it makes great demands and at the same time bestows astonishing gifts. Our ministry as leaders in the church is in a very real sense an impossible challenge. And yet if we attend to the who and the what, if we nurture both the heart and the mind, the strength we need for the challenges we face will come to us. By the grace of God, it will come.

Notes

CHAPTER 1

1. See Max DePree, *Leadership Is an Art* (New York: Doubleday, 1998), for an insightful discussion of the art of leadership.

2. Craig Dykstra, "The Pastoral Imagination," *Initiatives in Religion* 9, no. 1 (spring 2001): 1.

3. Dorothy C. Bass, ed., *Practicing Our Faith* (San Francisco: Jossey-Bass, 1998), 5.

4. Mark Yaconelli, "Focusing Youth Ministry through Christian Practices," in *Starting Right: Thinking Theologically about Youth Ministry*, Kenda Creasy Dean, Chap Clark, and Dave Rahn, eds. (Grand Rapids: Zondervan, 2001), 156.

5. Ibid., 56–62.

6. Ibid., 164.

7. Bass, *Practicing Our Faith*, 10.

8. Parker Palmer, *The Active Life* (San Francisco: Jossey-

Bass, 1990), 110. See 99–119 for an insightful discussion of the entire temptation story.

CHAPTER 2

1. Robert K. Greenleaf, "The Servant as Leader," in *Servant Leadership: A Journey into the Nature of Legitimate Power and Greatness* (New York: Paulist, 1997), 7.

2. Ibid., 15.

3. Included among those business leaders and writers who acknowledge their debt to Greenleaf are James Autry, *The Servant Leader: How to Build a Creative Team, Develop Great Morale and Improve Bottom-line Performance* (Roseville, Calif.: Prima Publishing, 2001); Warren Bennis, *On Becoming a Leader* (Cambridge, Mass.: Perseus Books, 1994); Stephen R. Covey, *Principle-Centered Leadership* (New York: Summit Books, 1991); Max DePree, *Leadership Is an Art* (East Lansing: Michigan State University Press, 1987); Peter Senge, *The Fifth Discipline: The Art and Practice of the Learning Organization* (New York: Doubleday/Currency, 1990); and Margaret Wheatley, *Leadership and the New Science: Discovering Order in a Chaotic World*, 2nd ed. (San Francisco: Berrett-Koehler, 1999).

4. For an illustration of his influence in nonprofit leadership see John Carver, *On Board Leadership: Selected Writings from the Creator of the World's Most Provocative and Systematic Governance Model* (San Francisco: Jossey-Bass, 2002). Illustrations from educational leadership can be seen in Parker Palmer, *The Courage to Teach* (San Francisco: Jossey-Bass, 1998), and Thomas J. Sergiovanni, *Moral Leadership: Getting to the Heart of School Improvement* (San Francisco: Jossey-Bass, 1992).

5. These Greenleaf essays are contained in Larry C. Spears, ed., *The Power of Servant Leadership* (San Francisco: Berrett-

Koehler, 1998). Another collection of Greenleaf's writings on the religious dimension of servant leadership can be found in Anne T. Fraker and Larry C. Spears, eds., *Seeker and Servant: Reflections on Religious Leadership* (San Francisco: Jossey-Bass, 1996).

6. Jane L. Fryer, *Servant Leadership: Setting Leaders Free* (St. Louis: Concordia, 2001), and Fryer, *Trust and Teams: Putting Servant Leadership to Work* (St. Louis: Concordia, 2002).

7. David S. Young, *Servant Leadership for Church Renewal: Shepherds by the Living Springs* (Scottsdale, Pa.: Herald Press, 1999).

8. Elizabeth O'Connor, *Servant Leaders, Servant Structures* (Washington: Servant Leadership School, 1991).

9. For examples of these critiques, see Susan Dunfee, *Beyond Servanthood: Christianity and the Liberation of Women* (Lantham, Md.: University Press of American, 1989); Jacquelyn Grant, "The Sin of Servanthood and the Deliverance of Discipleship," in *A Troubling in My Soul*, Emilie Townes, ed. (Maryknoll, N.Y.: Orbis, 1993); and Edward C. Zaragoza, *No Longer Servants, but Friends: A Theology of Ordained Ministry* (Nashville: Abingdon, 1999).

10. Greenleaf, *Servant Leadership*, 29.

11. Greenleaf, *The Power of Servant Leadership*, 85.

12. See Brian D. McLaren, *The Secret Message of Jesus: Uncovering the Truth That Could Change Everything* (Nashville: W Publishing, 2006), 46–49, for an insightful discussion of parables.

13. Robert E. Quinn, *Deep Change: Discovering the Leader Within* (San Francisco: Jossey-Bass, 1996), 3.

14. Ibid., 91.

15. Michael Fullan, *Leading in a Culture of Change* (San Francisco: Jossey-Bass, 2001), 33.

16. Ibid., 4. The book presents a detailed description of each of these components.

17. Ibid., 121.

18. See Ronald A. Heifetz, *Leadership without Easy Answers* (Cambridge, Mass.: Belknap Press, 1994), 73–76; and Ronald A. Heifetz and Marty Linsky, *Leadership on the Line: Staying Alive through the Dangers of Leading* (Boston: Harvard Business School Press, 2002), 13–15, for helpful discussions of the distinctions between technical and adaptive work.

19. See Heifetz and Linsky, *Leadership on the Line,* 123–39.

20. Daniel Goleman, Richard Boyatzis, and Annie McKee, *Primal Leadership: Realizing the Power of Emotional Intelligence* (Boston: Harvard Business School Press, 2002), 53–88, provides descriptions of each of these roles.

21. Ibid., 3.

22. Heifetz and Linsky, *Leadership on the Line,* 89.

23. Ibid.

CHAPTER 3

1. Rochelle Melander and Harold Eppley, *The Spiritual Leader's Guide to Self-Care* (Herndon, Va.: Alban Institute, 2002), xiii.

2. Heifetz and Linsky, *Leadership on the Line,* 163.

3. Ibid., 164.

4. Ibid., 185.

5. Ibid., 204.

6. Stephen R. Covey, *The Seven Habits of Highly Effective People* (New York: Simon & Schuster, 1989), 287.

7. Stephen R. Covey, *Principle-Centered Leadership* (New York: Simon & Schuster, 1991), 38.

8. Ibid., 302.

9. Robert Greenleaf, "Education and Maturity," in *The Power of Servant Leadership*, 62.

10. Ibid., 65.

11. Ibid., 67.

12. Ibid., 68.

13. Ibid.

14. Ibid., 71.

15. Ibid., 75.

16. Ibid., italics original.

17. Kirk Byron Jones, *Rest in the Storm: Self-Care Strategies for Clergy and Other Caregivers* (Valley Forge, Pa.: Judson, 2001), 6.

18. Jones, *Rest in the Storm*, 8.

19. Roy M. Oswald, *Clergy Self-Care: Finding a Balance for Effective Ministry* (Washington: Alban Institute, 1991), 17.

20. M. Shawn Copeland, "Saying Yes and Saying No," in Bass, *Practicing Our Faith*, 60.

21. Ibid., 66.

22. Oswald, *Clergy Self-Care*, 17.

23. Bill Lyon, *Philadelphia Inquirer*, September 9, 1997.

24. Jones, *Rest in the Storm*, 37.

25. Stephanie Paulsell, *Honoring the Body: Meditations on a Christian Practice* (San Francisco: Jossey-Bass, 2002), 7–8.

26. Parker J. Palmer, *Let Your Life Speak: Listening for the Voice of Vocation* (San Francisco: Jossey-Bass, 2000), 63.

27. Norman Shawchuck and Roger Heuser, *Leading the Congregation: Caring for Yourself While Serving the People* (Nashville: Abingdon, 1993), 29.

CHAPTER 4

1. Fullan, *Leading in a Culture of Change*, 130.

2. Goleman, Boyatzis, and McKee, *Primal Leadership*, 209.

3. Greenleaf, *Servant Leadership*, 15.

4. James M. Kouzes and Barry Z. Posner, *The Leadership Challenge*, 3rd ed. (San Francisco: Jossey-Bass, 2002), 14.

5. Ibid.

6. Ibid., 52.

7. See Covey, *Principle-Centered Leadership*, 190–201, for a discussion of all six characteristics.

8. Ibid., 196.

9. Ibid., 198.

10. Robert K. Greenleaf, *The Power of Servant Leadership*, edited by Larry C. Spears (San Francisco: Berrett-Koehler, 1998), 5–8.

11. Robert E. Quinn, *Deep Change: Discovering the Leader Within* (San Francisco: Jossey-Bass, 1996), 3.

12. Ibid., 34–35.

13. Ibid., 54.

14. Ibid., 78.

15. Ibid.

16. Ibid., 85.

17. William H. Willimon, *Pastor: The Theology and Practice of Ordained Ministry* (Nashville: Abingdon, 2002), 302.

18. Norman Shawchuck and Roger Heuser, *Leading the Congregation: Caring for Yourself While Serving the People* (Nashville: Abingdon, 1993), 124.

CHAPTER 5

1. Kouzes and Posner, *The Leadership Challenge*, 125.

2. Quinn, *Deep Change*, 43.

3. John P. Kotter, *Leading Change* (Boston: Harvard Business School Press, 1996), 68.

4. Peter M. Senge, *The Fifth Discipline: The Art and Practice of The Learning Organization* (New York: Doubleday, 1990), 206.

5. Jim Herrington, Mike Bonem, and James H. Furr, *Leading Congregational Change: A Practical Guide for the Transformational Journey* (San Francisco: Jossey-Bass, 2000), 50.

6. Ibid.

7. Ibid.

8. Senge, *The Fifth Discipline*, 209.

9. Kouzes and Posner, *The Leadership Challenge*, 130.

10. Kotter, *Leading Change*, 68–69, 72.

11. Herrington, Bonem, and Furr, *Leading Congregational*

Change, 49.

12. Greenleaf, *The Power of Servant Leadership,* 34.

13. Ibid., 35.

14. Ibid., 37.

15. Senge, *The Fifth Discipline,* 213.

16. Ibid., 218.

17. Kotter, *Leading Change,* 79.

18. Herrington, Bonem, and Furr, *Leading Congregational Change,* 52.

19. Ibid., 53.

20. Further insight into the use of discernment in congregations can be found in Suzanne G. Farnham, Stephanie A. Hull, and R. Taylor McLean, *Grounded in God: Listening Hearts Discernment for Group Deliberations,* revised ed. (Harrisburg, Pa.: Morehouse, 1999); Suzanne G. Farnham, Joseph P. Gill, R. Taylor McLean, and Susan M. Ward, *Listening Hearts: Discerning Call in Community* (Harrisburg, Pa.: Morehouse, 2002); and Danny E. Morris and Charles M. Olsen, *Discerning God's Will Together: A Spiritual Practice for the Church* (Nashville: Upper Room Books, 1997).

21. For a complete description of this concept see my book *Traveling Together: A Guide for Disciple-Forming Congregations* (Herndon, Va.: Alban Institute, 2005).

22. Quinn, *Deep Change,* 91.

CHAPTER 6

1. Max DePree, *Leadership Is an Art* (New York: Doubleday,

1989), 9.

2. Wesley Granberg-Michaelson, *Leadership from Inside Out: Spirituality and Organizational Change* (New York: Crossroad, 2004), 116.

3. Margaret Wheatley, *Leadership and the New Science: Discovering Order in a Chaotic World*, 2nd ed. (San Francisco: Berrett-Koehler, 1999), 130.

4. Kouzes and Posner, *The Leadership Challenge*, 81–83.

5. Ibid., 82.

6. Ibid., 94.

7. Ibid.

8. Ibid., 91.

9. Ibid., 155.

10. Greenleaf, *The Power of Servant Leadership*, 138.

11. Ibid.

12. Robert Kegan and Lisa Laskow Lahey, *How the Way We Talk Can Change the Way We Work* (San Francisco: Jossey-Bass, 2001), 7.

13. Ibid., 32.

14. Ibid., 75.

15. Ibid., 79.

16. Ibid., 99.

17. Ibid., 98.

18. Ibid., 111.

19. Ibid., 128.

20. Kouzes and Posner, *The Leadership Challenge*, 88.

21. Ibid., 361.

22. Ibid., 363.

23. Ibid., 99–100.

24. DePree, *Leadership Is an Art*, 72.

25. Ibid., 80.

26. Scott Cormode, *Making Spiritual Sense: Christian Leaders as Spiritual Interpreters* (Nashville: Abingdon Press, 2006), xi.

27. Ibid., 9.

28. Ibid., 14.

29. Ibid., 47.

30. Ibid., 63.

31. Ibid., 82.

32. Ibid., 65.

33. Ibid.

34. Ibid., 66.

35. Ibid., 88.

36. Ibid., 92.

CHAPTER 7

1. See Loren Mead, *The Once and Future Church: Reinventing the Congregation for a New Mission Frontier* (Bethesda: Alban Institute, 1991), and Mead, *Five Challenges for the Once and Future Church* (Bethesda: Alban Institute, 1996).

2. See Bill Easum, *Sacred Cows Make Gourmet Burgers: Ministry Anytime, Anywhere, by Anyone* (Nashville:

Abingdon, 1995).

3. Parker Palmer, *The Active Life: A Spirituality of Work, Creativity and Caring* (San Francisco: Jossey-Bass, 1990), 109.

4. Ibid., 111.

5. Ibid., 109.

6. Kouzes and Posner, *The Leadership Challenge,* 288.

7. Ibid., 281.

8. Ibid., 279–301.

9. Quinn, *Deep Change,* 223.

10. Ibid., 225.

11. Ibid., 227.

12. Ibid., 228.

13. Goleman et al., *Primal Leadership,* 110.

14. Kotter, *Leading Change,* 102.

15. Jeffrey D. Jones, *Traveling Together: A Guide for Disciple-Forming Congregations* (Herndon, Va.: Alban Institute, 2006).

16. Dick Broholm and John Hoffman, *Empowering Laity for Their Full Ministry: Nine Blocking/Enabling Forces* (Newton Centre, Mass.: Andover Newton Laity Project, 1981).

17. Ibid., "Gifts and Call," 2.

18. Ibid., "Content of Ministry," 2.

19. Ibid., "Spiritual Formation," 3.

20. Ibid., "Language and Liturgy," 2.

21. Ibid., "Validation," 2.

22. Ibid., "Roles and Structures," 1.

23. Ibid., "Roles and Structures," 2.

24. Ibid., "Education," 2.

25. Ibid., "Content of Ministry," 1.

26. Kouzes and Posner, *The Leadership Challenge*, 295.

CHAPTER 8

1. Kouzes and Posner, *The Leadership Challenge*, 244.

2. Ibid., 247.

3. Ibid., 248.

4. Susan A. Wheelan, *Creating Effective Teams: A Guide for Members and Leaders* (Thousand Oaks, Calif.: Sage Publications, 1999), 111.

5. Ibid., 26.

6. Covey, *Principle-Centered Leadership*, 171.

7. Quinn, *Deep Change*, 161.

8. Kouzes and Posner, *The Leadership Challenge*, 251.

9. Fran Rees, *How to Lead Teams* (San Francisco: Jossey-Bass, 1991), 41.

10. Ibid., 39–41.

11. Wheelan, *Creating Effective Teams*, 42–43.

12. Rees, *How to Lead Teams*, 20.

13. Ibid., 21.

14. Wheelan, *Creating Effective Teams*, 75.

15. Goleman et al., *Primal Leadership*, 175.

16. Ibid., 176.

17. C. Jeff Wood, *Congregational Megatrends* (Herndon, Va.: Alban Institute, 1996), 136.

18. Ibid., 135.

19. Thomas G. Bandy, *Kicking Habits: Welcome Relief for Addicted Churches, Upgrade Edition* (Nashville: Abingdon, 2001), 151.

20. See Joseph R. Myers, *The Search to Belong: Rethinking Intimacy, Community and Small Groups* (Grand Rapids: Zondervan, 2003), for an interesting and insightful discussion of belonging.

21. Jeffrey Arnold, *The Big Book on Small Groups* (Downers Grove, Ill.: InterVarsity Press, 1992), 35.

22. Corinne Ware, *Connecting to God: Nurturing Spirituality through Small Groups* (Herndon, Va.: Alban Institute, 1997), 2.

23. Charles Olsen, *Transforming Church Boards into Communities of Spiritual Leaders* (Herndon, Va.: Alban Institute, 1995), 20–25.

24. Ibid., 93.

25. A number of books provide helpful insights for more formal training of group leaders and the development of a small group ministry. Among these are Jeffrey Arnold, *The Big Book on Small Groups Book* (Downers Grove, Ill.: InterVarsity Press, 1992); Jeffrey Arnold, *Starting Small Groups* (Nashville: Abingdon, 1997); Nill Donohue and Russ Robinson, *Building a Church of Small Groups* (Grand Rapids: Zondervan, 2001); Dale Galloway, *The Small Groups Book* (Grand Rapids: Fleming Revell, 1995); Robert L. Hill, *The Complete Guide to Small Group Ministry: Saving the World Ten at a Time* (Boston: Skinner House Books, 2003); Thomas G. Kirkpatrick, *Small Groups in the Church: A Handbook for Creating Community* (Herndon, Va.: Alban

Institute, 1995); Neal F. McBride, *How to Build a Small Groups Ministry* (Colorado Springs: NAVPress, 1995); and Corinne Ware, *Connecting to God* (Herndon, Va.: Alban Institute, 1997).

26. Kouzes and Posner, *The Leadership Challenge*, 247.

CHAPTER 9

1. See, for example, Charles H. Cosgrove and Dennis D. Hatfield, *Church Conflict: The Hidden Systems Behind the Fights* (Nashville: Abingdon, 1994); Norma C. Everist, *Church Conflict: From Contention to Collaboration* (Nashville: Abingdon, 2004); Roger Fisher and William Ury, *Getting to Yes: Negotiating Agreement without Giving In* (New York: Penguin, 1991); Speed B. Leas, *Discover Your Conflict Management Style* (Herndon, Va.: Alban Institute, 1997); Speed B. Leas, *Moving Your Church through Conflict* (Herndon, Va.: Alban Institute, 1996); and David B. Lott, ed., *Conflict Management in Congregations* (Herndon, Va.: Alban Institute, 2001).

2. Goleman et al., *Primal Leadership*, 256.

3. Heifetz and Linsky, *Leadership on the Line*, 101.

4. Kotter, *Leading Change*, 40.

5. Ibid., 36.

6. Ibid., 44.

7. Fullan, *Leading in a Culture of Change*, 74.

8. Ibid.

9. Heifetz and Linsky, *Leadership on the Line*, 102.

10. Heifetz, *Leadership without Easy Answers*, 106.

11. These guidelines are briefly described in Heifetz, *Leadership without Easy Answers*, 128, and illustrated throughout the book, and in Heifetz and Linsky, *Leadership on the Line*.

12. Heifetz and Linsky, *Leadership on the Line*, 109.

13. Heifetz, *Leadership without Easy Answers*, 128.

14. Ibid., 263.

15. Heifetz and Linsky, *Leadership on the Line*, 188.

16. Heifetz, *Leadership without Easy Answers*, 263.

17. Heifetz and Linsky, *Leadership on the Line*, 192.

18. Ibid., 198.

19. Kouzes and Posner, *The Leadership Challenge*, 219.

20. Ibid.

21. Ibid., 220.

22. Heifetz, *Leadership without Easy Answers*, 107.